"A critical and compelling discussion of how living in the digital age affects our minds, bodies, and relationships—and, most importantly, how, through the simple practice of mindfulness, we can navigate these times with clarity and wisdom."

TARA BRACH, PHD
author of *Radical Acceptance: Embracing Your Life with the Heart of a Buddha*
and *True Refuge: Finding Peace & Freedom in Your Own Awakened Heart*

"I like to think that my life is rooted in contemplative presence, that I am not one of those people so enamored of social media and virtual reality that I define myself by my Facebook profile or feel lost without my smartphone. So imagine my shock when I read *The Power of Off* and nodded my head in recognition on every page. How could I have let this happen? But this book is not only a diagnosis of the addiction to technology that plagues us; it is a wise and loving remedy, a lucid invitation to mindful living, that is, re-inhabiting the heart of life itself. Nancy Colier showed me the off button, and I am grateful."

MIRABAI STARR
author of *God of Love: A Guide to the Heart of Judaism, Christianity & Islam*
and *Caravan of No Despair: A Memoir of Loss & Transformation*

"Timely, topical, and most of all thoughtful, Nancy Colier offers unique insight and deeper questions as we wrestle with what it means to be human and connected in the digital age."

CHRISTOPHER WILLARD, PSYD
author of *Growing Up Mindful: Essential Practices to Help Children, Teens, and Families Find Balance, Calm, and Resilience*

"Nancy Colier's *The Power of Off* is an intelligently written awakening to the addictive nature of our beloved, ever present, personal technology. In these illuminating and well-researched pages the reader will find him/herself 'busted' spending endless hours staring/playing/interacting with one device or another. While the jury is not in as yet regarding the societal effects modern technology will have on us and our children, one thing Ms. Colier makes clear is that our addiction to these miniature marvels is wrought with potential social and developmental issues. Her well-thought-out and constructive suggestions and pragmatic practices are insightful and laden with positive potential. Highly recommended."

ALLAN LOKOS
founder/guiding teacher of The Community Meditation Center in New York City and author of *Pocket Peace, Patience*, and *Through the Flames*

"In this increasingly chaotic and technologically saturated world, *The Power of Off* is a desperately needed offering. Complete with self-evaluation tools, remedies for disconnection, and mindfulness practices, Nancy Colier guides us back to feeling nourished and grounded as human beings."

CHRIS GROSSO
author of *Indie Spiritualist* and *Everything Mind*

the power of off

the power of off

THE MINDFUL WAY
TO STAY SANE
IN A VIRTUAL WORLD

nancy colier

SOUNDS TRUE
BOULDER, COLORADO

Sounds True
Boulder, CO 80306

Published 2016

Cover design by Rachael Murray
Book design by Beth Skelley

Printed in the United States of America

Library of Congress Cataloging-in-Publication Data
Names: Colier, Nancy, author.
Title: The power of off : the mindful way to stay sane in a virtual world /
   Nancy Colier.
Description: Boulder, CO : Sounds True, [2017]
Identifiers: LCCN 2016022006 | ISBN 9781622037957 (pbk.)
Subjects: LCSH: Information technology—Psychological aspects. |
   Information technology—Social aspects. | Attention. | Self-control. |
   Mindfulness (Psychology)
Classification: LCC HM851 .C635 2017 | DDC 302.2—dc23
LC record available at https://lccn.loc.gov/2016022006

Ebook ISBN 978-1-62203-796-4

10 9 8 7 6 5 4 3 2 1

for juliet and gretchen

contents

PART 3 Our Relationship with Ourselves

PART 4 Creating Space—Inside and Out

introduction

finding ground in a virtual world

T he most important thing is to find out what is the most important thing," said Zen monk Shunryu Suzuki Roshi.[1] Every day, when I wake up, I try to remember to ask myself: *What is the most important thing? What is my heart's longing? What parts of myself do I want to nourish and grow? What do I want to offer?* In essence, *What really matters?*

Every day I try to touch into what this astounding experience of being alive is really about. The contemplation of the most important thing keeps me connected to my most sincere and profound longings and my deeper wisdom. When I am grounded in what is most important, I am more discerning in my choices, less likely to be swayed off course by my small-minded aspects, and far more likely to finish the day feeling good.

As a psychotherapist, interfaith minister, and spiritual counselor, I spend my days talking with people about their lives, internal and external. While functioning successfully in the world, many of those I meet with report a sense of overwhelm, of being consumed by the distractions and chronic multitasking that technology makes possible and to some degree necessary. Whether we're tinkering on social media, Googling old acquaintances, looking up facts on Wikipedia, or updating and learning new software, we are spending far too much of our time doing things that don't really matter to us. At this moment in history, as a result of the new opportunities and demands that technology creates, we have forgotten not only *what is most important* but also that we need to ask ourselves that question. Why do so many people describe the feeling of being disconnected from what really matters, from what makes us feel nourished and grounded as human beings? And, most importantly, how do we remember not to forget to ask, *What really matters?*

What is real and what is virtual are shifting as technology explodes into our daily lives. At the same time, we are transforming as a society and a species. *What is the most important thing?* seems like a question in transition. But is it really?

Because of my profession, I have a front-row seat from which to witness, investigate, and try to understand the metamorphosis that we human beings are undergoing. And I am not just a witness to but also an inhabitant of this brave new world, experiencing the effects of technology on myself, my children, my friends, my clients, and all others in my life. We are all facing new issues and difficulties as a result of our use of and reliance on technology. We are changing emotionally, relating to one another and ourselves in profoundly different ways than we did before the technology explosion. How we spend our time, what motivates us, what we want—all are on a radical course of transformation. In many cases, the adaptations that are occurring work well for technology. By the second, technology is growing and evolving into something we can't live without. But is technology helping us humans to grow, emotionally, intellectually, and spiritually? Or do we need to alter our relationship with technology so that we humans can also continue to evolve?

I observe more and more of my clients, as well as friends, family, and others, becoming dependent on their devices in order to feel complete, "calm," and basically okay. Many people now need their devices and the ongoing infusion of entertainment, information, and communication that technology provides to keep themselves from feeling bored and agitated, which are now considered the normal sensations for a life that is "turned off." What we expect from the present moment has changed: we are now accustomed to ongoing stimulation and feel anxious and lacking without it. There is a continual sense that we *should* be doing something, which then causes us to grab our smartphones to seek some relief from that anxiety. And while most people now check their smartphones 150 times per day, or every six minutes,[2] not enough of us consider our behavior around technology to be a real problem.

Over a relatively short span of time, our use of technology has exploded—smartphones, mobile devices, tablets, social and other media, emails, texting, apps, games, music, videos, photo sharing, and all the rest. Technology has become a persistent presence in our public and private worlds, day and night. The average person now spends more than eight hours a day on their phone and laptop, more time than they spend sleeping, and most have their phones turned on all the time, even in bed.[3] And young adults are now sending an average of 110 texts per day.[4] But perhaps more remarkable even than how much our use of technology is increasing is how we are relating to it. On that front, 46 percent of smartphone users now say that their devices are something they "couldn't live without."[5]

With the assistance of technology, we now have the ability to know, do, watch, and learn almost anything. But by indulging that ability, we have created a state in which every nook and cranny of our internal and external space is filled with stuff to do, think about, watch, listen to, know, and learn. Our internal hard drives are jammed beyond capacity with thoughts, information, and new tasks. People I meet with, work with, live with, and everything else with consistently report a great longing for space, room to breathe, time with themselves, or, as we now call it, "bandwidth"—and yet such peace, quiet, and downtime are harder and harder to find or create. Our lives are filled with more possibilities than ever before to connect, consume, and discover—all good things—but in the face of these possibilities, we are also feeling less connected, less centered, and less satisfied. The digital age is an age of both too much and not enough.

How do we stay in touch with what is most important to us when we're buried under hundreds of emails and texts and technological tasks each day? How do we stay in the present moment in a society that beckons us with relentless—and enticing—distractions? How do we maintain connection in our relationships when conversations are interrupted dozens of times and so many people are busy staring into their personal screens? Where do we find the silence and focus we need when there is almost nowhere left to escape from the chimes, bells, and vibrations that constantly invade our private spaces, when every activity is part of a larger multitasking operation? With what skills can we stay empowered and calm when we must continually figure out how to keep our technology running smoothly just so we can participate in the world? How do we hold onto a sense of tangible reality when so much of our life is virtual? And, most importantly, how do we stay grounded and connected to our deeper wisdom at this time in history, on this wild digital ride that the human race has embarked upon? How do we live peacefully with the excitement and madness and do it all without going mad ourselves?

I recently watched a woman almost run down by a taxi because she was so focused on her smartphone she didn't notice she was standing in the middle of the street. Two men pulled her out of harm's way at the last moment. When she made it to the other side of the street, she got right back to her device, as if nothing had just happened. She was not fazed by the event, at least not enough to interrupt her flow of texting or even to thank the two men who saved her life. Technology is a powerful tool for communication, and yet the way we are using it and the authority we are awarding it are also making it into a powerful impediment to our sense of presence and awareness.

We are succumbing to our more primitive tendencies toward unconsciousness, going under a kind of technological anesthesia, which renders us unaware of where we actually are physically and with whom we are sharing company. Technology is dazzling us into a form of entertaining sleep, and too many of us are not yet making conscious choices about whether we agree with what is happening and in fact want to disappear from our lives.

Technology offers the potential for everything we can imagine, but when we do make the effort to get quiet, we often discover that what we really want, "the most important thing," is to experience a good life, one filled with contentment, love, meaning, and depth, a life filled with rich experiences and relationships—not more of everything virtually possible. Technology, as too many of us are now using it, is not leading us to a better life, not to a state of fundamental well-being.

In today's world, our digitally marinated minds must decide what our hearts and spirits need in order to be well—and thus what nourishment we will draw from life. A digitally marinated mind, however, is not the right candidate for this task because the amped-up, teched-out mind is not only out of touch with the heart and spirit, it also has a radically different agenda and set of needs. When our technology-fueled mind is consulted as if it were a wise sage, it convinces us that the following falsehoods are true:

- The more virtual friends and followers we acquire, the more connected and loved we will feel.

- The more "likes" we get for our opinions and ideas, the more liked we will feel, and the more we will like ourselves.

- The more we communicate, the less alone we will feel.

- The more entertainment we consume, the less bored and empty we will feel.

- The more information we amass, the more interesting life—and we—will become.

- The easier we make our lives, the better they will be.

- If other people know about our lives, our lives will feel more real to us.

- If the world knows who we are, we will know who we are.

- With enough virtual destinations to choose from, we will find somewhere that we want to be.

- We must keep up with technology if we do not want to be left behind and miss out on life.

But as much as our world is in flux, what human beings need to feel grounded, connected, and satisfied has not changed. At a deeper level, the stuff and noise that our devices offer do not satisfy. For all of technology's benefits, it is not our missing piece, not what will make our existences meaningful. We need to ground the monkey—that is, bring our monkey mind back into connection with our heart, our deepest truths, and what is truly important to us.

What do we need in order to be able to inhabit our lives peacefully and joyfully? Here are the leading contenders:

- To be aware and present—to show up for our lives

- To feel emotionally connected to ourselves and others

- To feel cared about, valued, and known

- To feel engaged in a life of meaning

- To feel we have choice and control

- To feel we are part of something larger than ourselves

- To live an authentic life—a life that is in sync with who we truly are and what really matters to us

Waking Up

Humans and technology are now in an intimate relationship—sharing a bed, literally. Technology, because of its ease and mobility, accompanies us everywhere, like a limb, in a way that it never could before. Our smartphones come with us into the bedroom (90 percent of eighteen- to twenty-nine-year-olds sleep with their smartphones), onto the toilet, into the shower, to meals, weddings, funerals . . . everywhere we go, they go.[6] The fact that we never have to be without our devices means that we never *are* without them, and we increasingly mistrust that we can be okay without them. Since we are now attached, we need to figure out a way to make this relationship a healthy one. Now more than ever, we need to cultivate mindfulness in our lives so that we can be guided by our own wisdom and intelligence and not be dragged around by the bright lights of technology, tossing virtual paper into virtual wastebaskets and popping virtual bubble wrap. We need the wisdom of mindfulness to put us back into our lives, so that we're not lost somewhere else while our life is happening. After all, we are not virtual. We need more than a jack and a charger to stay connected to life.

It is alarming to see us choosing to use technology in ways that indulge a proclivity for unconsciousness. But what is even more alarming is that we have shifted our relationship with technology so that it is no longer just a tool that we control, something we set aside when it doesn't help. We have crossed a threshold and are now surrendering our authority and experience to technology as if it were the master and we its slaves. Because technology can do something, we think it should—must do it, in fact—without considering whether we actually want it to or whether it even makes sense.

The scientist is delighted and proud when he discovers that by offering food as a reward for pushing a lever, she can get her rat, an otherwise mindless subject, to behave exactly as she wants. The scientist can control her subject, at least at first. But soon, what the scientist doesn't know is that the rat is on to her game. "Look at the fool, I can get her to feed me whenever I want," the rat squeaks to his other rat friends. So who's in charge now, technology or humans? We have created a relationship with technology in which, more and more, we are the ones feeding it on demand, awarding it a life force and intelligence unto itself, while we continue to imagine that we are in control.

Every new scientific and technological innovation throughout history has led to massive changes in society, but this shift in who's in charge is what makes this technological revolution profoundly different from any we've yet known. Ultimately, if we surrender all our authority to technology, as if it were an animate entity, it would not just change society; it would also change who we fundamentally are as human beings.

This book is meant to sound the call for wakefulness, more loudly than any ringtone can ring—to create a handshake between technology and our basic humanness, to remind us how to use technology in a way that promotes true well-being, and to encourage and empower us to live from our wisdom rather than our impulses. This book is about raising consciousness at a time when our society is undergoing an epidemic of unconsciousness. It's about finding ground in a world that is increasingly untethered and ephemeral. It's about nurturing depth even as shallowness threatens to become the norm. This book is a call to reclaim the right to be masters of our lives at a time in history when we are giving that power away.

My intention is to help you remember "the most important thing" while living with and making use of technology. This book offers a road map back to here, not the concept of "the present moment," but the direct experience of it, inside your body, heart, and mind—and, I hope, an experience of living that is infused with the full richness that life offers.

Awakening: The Only Way *To* Is *Through*

I am going to take you on a journey in these pages. My hope is that we can travel together through unconsciousness into consciousness, through distraction into presence, and through the enslavement of mind to the freedom of mindfulness. I say "through" because in the end the only way through is through. We can't skip over the place we are—on our way to somewhere better.

Some of the challenges and alienation that I point to in our new digital world are caused directly by the use and prevalence of technology, while others are inherent aspects of human nature that technology enables and exacerbates. Although helpful in many ways, unfortunately technology also makes it far easier for us to act on, and thus has the potential to strengthen and support, our more escapist and unconscious tendencies. Technology facilitates the natural human drive to flee from the moment, avoid what's challenging, and seek pleasure at all costs, none of which create happiness, peace, or well-being in the end. My hope with this book is that it will reawaken our more evolved aspects, the wisdom, compassion, and desire for growth that are equally part of our basic nature.

By exploring the ways in which we are using technology to indulge our more immature and undiscerning tendencies, my intention is to reroute and reawaken us into a more satisfying, nourishing, and ultimately profound experience of our own existence. By examining the ways we are turning technology into an active and personified entity with its own sovereignty, I mean to help us recapture our fundamental intelligence and independence. In the process of looking into and experiencing our drives for distraction, passivity, unconsciousness, and immediate gratification, however, we may have to ride through some uncomfortable feelings. The path to freedom includes being able to investigate painful truths about ourselves and the willingness to uncover our primitive and even unappealing aspects, all of which require a fierceness and courage from you, my reader. To create a new way of feeling and behaving, a new kind of life, we need to be honest about how we are feeling and behaving right now, about what kind of life we are really living.

This is not a book about the concept of technological addiction or any imaginary user. Quite the contrary: it is about you and your personal experience, the quality of your life, what is important, and how you want to live and thrive. Do you personally need to address your use of and relationship with technology? The truth is always the best launching point for change. In honor of the truth, let's begin, then, by taking the following assessment:

- Do you want to cut down on your device use but find you are unable to do so?

- Do you feel negative emotions—such as agitation, irritation, depression, anger, exasperation, boredom, et cetera—when you can't use your device?

- Have real-world activities—such as hobbies, sports, community involvement, reading books, learning, and so forth—decreased as a result of your time spent online?

- Has your time online negatively impacted your job or education?

- Have your social relationships in the real world diminished or suffered as a result of your online behavior?

- Has your physical or emotional health suffered because of your technology use—for example, have you experienced loss of sleep, decrease in exercise, eye strain, back or neck aches, muscle pain, carpal tunnel syndrome, finger twitching, anxiety, stress, blood pressure, exhaustion, or the like?

- Do you ever feel guilty, uncomfortable, or otherwise bad about the amount of time you spend on your devices?

- Do you ever feel guilty, uncomfortable, or otherwise bad about behavior that results from your online use?

- Do you ever use your work as an excuse to be online?

- Do you ever lie about your online use?

- Do you crave a more meaningful life and believe that technology may get in the way of it?

If you answered yes to just one of these questions, it is possible you are addicted. If you answered yes to two questions, you are probably addicted, and if you answered yes to three or more questions, you are almost certainly addicted.

Again, to get to a better *there*, we need to start here, in this *now*. That said, if you choose to come along for this ride, begin by honoring your courage to do so. And if now is not the right time for this journey, honor your truth. What I can assure you of is that, though it might be uncomfortable to stay with this process during some moments, the place where you are headed, your ultimate destination—to freedom of awareness, the joy of presence, the magic of mindfulness, the power to choose how you want to live your own life—is well worth your effort.

One last note: Throughout these chapters, I raise a number of questions, invitations, really, to investigate your own experience. It is important to take the time to contemplate these questions, not just breeze through them as if they are mere interesting intellectual ponderings. Notice how the inquiries apply and resonate, what they spark in you. And beyond contemplating and noticing, I encourage you to journal about what you discover in the process. These inquiries are meant to be exercises that require your attention and effort—that is, if you genuinely want to create or even just to investigate change.

And—Not But

This is a book about how we humans are using and relating to technology—not the technology that flies planes, assists surgeries, or makes life better in so many ways, but rather the sort that occupies many people's attention most of the day. You could call it "relational technology": smartphones, email, social media, gaming, and all their cousins. *The Power of Off* examines the challenges that technology is creating for us and how it is leading us away from feeling present, feeling connected to ourselves, and, in a word, feeling well.

In therapy, when someone talks about the difficulties they have with a parent, we examine their experience in the larger context of the entire relationship, which most of the time also includes deep love and attachment. The reason the suffering feels so intense is precisely because the love and attachment are so intense. In the end, everything resolves in contradiction. With technology, too, we need to learn to live from a place of *and*, not *but*: technology *and* a good life, as opposed to a good life *but* technology. Technology is a part of life now. It has the potential to create profound good in the world, to change lives for the better. It also helps us with the little things, as it did just this morning, when I was able to use the Internet to track down a particular doorknob I needed. But the benefits of technology are not the focus of this particular book. Suffice it to say, technology makes things better for us and also worse. Both are true, which is precisely why the issue is so complex.

When I speak of "technology" encouraging, leading, hypnotizing, influencing, causing, and essentially doing something to us—changing us—I do not mean to imply that our smartphones actually jump out of their cases and dangle pocket watches in front of our eyes while forcing us to play apps. When I use the term "technology," I am referring to the ways in which we are using and relating to technology. As with everything, we human beings are solely responsible for what we do with and how we relate to what we create. If our devices were left to their own devices, they would remain sleeping in their rhinestone cases. It is not the devices that need to wake up in the digital age, but, rather, we human beings.

PART
1

our relationship
with technology

1

the prison of availability

One of my clients is a television news producer in his late twenties. He comes into his therapy sessions every week with two smartphones. He places one on each arm of the chair he sits in. Throughout our sessions, the devices light up at least ten times (between the two), if not more. He glances down at his technology a minimum of once per minute. We talk about his need to keep the phones on and to always be available to what messages might be coming in from the office. He is aware that such behavior increases his state of anxiety and keeps him from being able to be fully present in his sessions or anywhere else. Still, he does not feel it is in his power to turn the phones off, not even during his therapy. He believes that his profession requires and deserves his attention around the clock and that if he is not available when a new story comes in, he could potentially miss out on an opportunity to make a name for himself in his professional world. The next story could be the one that rockets him to producer stardom. Furthermore, if something happens on a story that he's already covering, he believes he is the only one who can take care of what needs to be done. He has come to view himself as fundamentally irreplaceable, even for fifty minutes, in the process of the news being reported properly.

Another client recently interviewed for a job with an executive in the marketing industry. The executive explained that if she were to get the job as his assistant, it would mean that she would have to keep her phone on 24/7 and be constantly available to the needs of the job. This included sleep time, bathroom visits, and, of course, holidays. She was never to be without or even out of sight of her phone. While it may sound extreme, for people starting out in careers these days, uninterrupted availability is the assumed expectation of many employers—and what employees demand of themselves as well. When an employer provides a cell phone to an employee, there is an assumption that the employee will be available to answer it. The line between work life and personal life is now blurred. As Arnold Bakker, a professor of work and organizational psychology at Erasmus University Rotterdam, framed it, "The smartphone is the Trojan horse through which work sneaks into the home."[1] Even for those who have solidly established professions or for whom technology makes working remotely a much-appreciated option, still, constant connectivity and überavailability are now the norm and not the exception.

It is not just our professions to which we believe we must remain überavailable in the age of technology. As parents, we feel that we must be relentlessly on call to our children's needs. One woman I know takes every FaceTime request from her child, regardless of what she is doing. The fact that her child wants to be with her (on technology) means that she *should* make herself available. When many of the parents I know consider powering off for a moment, they are stymied by such thoughts as *What if it's my child really wanting or even needing me at the other end of that ding? What if it's that time when something really bad has happened?*

I notice that, like the news producer, the mothers of young children (and older children too) no longer turn their phones off during their therapy sessions. While they don't generally leave them in full view, nonetheless the phones are there, chiming softly inside their bags and being attended to when they do ring—just in case. "Just in case," in fact, has become the new guiding principle by which most parents live. We can't *not* be available now that technology has gifted us with the *possibility* of being available. To be unavailable when we could be available would be, as one mother put it, neglectful. The idea of our child receiving a voicemail and not our direct and immediate attention has become synonymous with abandonment.

Before mobile devices made around-the-clock communication possible and expected, it was generally only in the case of life or death, when a relative or other person close to us was sick, that we made ourselves unceasingly available, staying close to the phone at all times, just in case it might bring news. It was in the face of a potential emergency that we felt it necessary to live in a state of hyperreadiness, to be on call without a break. What's different now is that we are living in this state of hyperreadiness around the clock. In fact, we are not only living this way, we believe that we must live this way. As one friend explained, "The biggest fear when my smartphone goes dead is that everyone will think I'm receiving what they're sending me, regardless of whether I respond." When someone sends a text, there is an assumption that we are reading it right then, the instant it appears. (Of course, our phone *is* on, and we *are* checking it!) This assumption makes many of us feel like we have to do something with or about every communication that lands on our screen—reward the sender immediately with the flashing dots of our on-the-way response.

The definition of "being available" is being able to be used or obtained, to be at someone's disposal. Our basic state is now one of being at someone or something else's disposal without pause. Unfortunately, relentless availability creates relentless stress. Most of us know the anxiety we experience when someone we love is ill and we are on alert, constantly waiting. We now live that stress, to some degree, all the time, and it is as damaging as a situational, short-term state of acute stress. Actually, in some ways it is worse, because the demand for hyperavailability never eases and the situation that requires such availability is never resolved. We never get that phone call that allows us to finally stop listening for it. As one woman I know put it, "It's like never quite being finished with the job, whatever that job may be." Our new resting state is one that doesn't allow for real rest; a part of us must remain always at the ready, as if about to leap out of the starting gate. Although we may have gotten used to it, and thus not notice it as abnormal or even uncomfortable, we are living in what is really an ongoing fight or flight state.

It is important that we remember we are human beings and not robots. Unlike robots, we need to experience rest, but rest with consciousness and not just rest when we are asleep. We need time to be awake but *not* ready and available—to our boss, clients, partner, friends, and even our children. Even the busiest, most responsible, indispensable, or in-demand person can create small spaces to step off the hamster wheel of others' needs. When we award ourselves the opportunity to turn off the access button to the rest of the world, we experience a profound reduction in stress, not just on a mental level but also on a cellular level. Being fully off duty allows us to reboot our own systems, both body and mind. We need this kind of rest to reestablish well-being and, indeed, to be truly available during those times when we claim to be available.

It's a vicious cycle: the more available we become, the more we believe we must be available. The belief itself is a part of the very system that creates it. Here are some other beliefs:

- We can't be important in life and to others on just a part-time basis.

- Time by ourselves is time taken away from those who need us.

- Our level of importance is directly proportionate to the level of our availability.

- If we aren't there when people need us, we won't be needed.

- We never have enough time.

- We'll rest when we're dead.

These are the new truths by which we measure ourselves and our lives. We have created and locked ourselves inside a prison of inescapable effort.

While many of us do not believe that we have the choice to make ourselves unavailable, periodically we are aware that hyperavailability makes us feel tired, harried, and burned out. To escape the demands of perpetual availability, two women I know take breaks by cruising the high seas. In both cases, it's not because they particularly love ships or sailing, but because they feel that out in the middle of the sea is the only place where they are entitled to be unreachable, the vastness of the ocean between them and the rest of the world somehow providing them with the permission they need.

People try to cope with the demands of constant availability in all sorts of ways. Some people deal with availability stress by becoming more reliant on substances. The substance provides them with a sense of calm and offers an invitation to live more in line with their *wants* and not their *shoulds*.

In addition to substance use, relentless availability causes some people to disconnect from their own feelings. They walk around like emotional robots, answering every phone call, text, and email on a moment's notice, never stopping to ask if this kind of life is working for them or how they feel being constantly on call. It seems that the only way some people can bear the demands of availability is to turn themselves off to the actual experience of what it's like to have to be so available, to behave as if it's normal to be a twenty-four-hour service provider. When we react in this way, we succeed to some degree in avoiding the stress, dissatisfaction, and overwhelm we are carrying, but in so doing, we also turn away from our own hearts and real truth. We cannot live a fully joyful (or aware) life when we are shut down to a primary part of our life experience.

But rather than finding more ways to cope with the demands of availability, we ought to be focusing on whether we agree with such demands—those of others, society in general, and our newly conditioned selves. Rather than blindly accepting that we have to live this way, we ought to be examining the very belief system out of which our compliance arises.

There is a particular kind of relaxation experience that is a direct result of and only achieved by the act of bringing our attention to the present moment only, just this one singular moment—that is, not having our attention scattered in one hundred different directions at once. It is precisely the opposite of the stress, fatigue, and depressive symptoms that arise with heavy technology use.[2] When invited to be in just one place at one time, just here, we experience a sense of calm presence available to *only* this moment. However, being present requires that all of us be here now, not merely a piece of us. We experience presence when we give ourselves permission to land where we are completely and not keep a part of ourselves separate and reserved for what might come in from the outside. Ironically, although we demand of ourselves that we be available at all times—to everyone else and to the world at large—we do not provide ourselves with the same availability we believe everyone else deserves. We do not hold ourselves at the same level of importance as we hold all others.

Instead, we need to bring awareness to the new demands on our availability, recognize the effects that hyperreadiness has on us, and invoke the courage to decide *for ourselves* how available we actually want to be, when, and to whom. Even soldiers at war, men and women in true emergencies, are awarded the right to be, sometimes, *at ease*. Such a need is not a selfish demand but a biological desire and a vital building block in the creation of internal equanimity, as well as a requirement for basic mental and physical health.

Right now, stop what you are doing for just a moment. Can you feel this breath? And then the next one? And the next? See if you can take three conscious breaths, right now. Feel the breath directly in your body, entering and exiting. While turning off our phone is one path to breaking the stress of chronic availability, we can also find relief through a simple dip into our breath or into any of the body's senses. When we take a single conscious breath, or pause to feel the sensations in our body or to listen to the sounds coming into our ears, we turn the tables on perpetual availability and become available to ourselves in the deepest way. Diving into our own present-moment awareness, through the breath, through the senses, is the most simple and direct medicine for the condition of constant availability. Try it now: enter your body's experience, arrive here, and make yourself fully available to you.

In addition to conscious breathing (or sensing), try the following: schedule a time today to spend fifteen minutes being unreachable, entirely. If it helps to tell those who might want to contact you that you will be unavailable, do so. Notice the sensations in your body when you are unavailable, as well as the thoughts and feelings that arise. Don't react or judge. Just notice what is happening inside you in this off-duty space. If possible, practice this on a daily basis.

2

slaves to technology

recently bought a house. The house, I was told as I was signing the contract, was not just a house, but a *smart house*. I didn't know what that meant at the time, not really, but I wasn't concerned, because I'm pretty tech smart myself. What I now understand is that the translation for *smart house* is "dumb human." I have now participated in at least a dozen conversations and three run-throughs with realtors and the previous owner, all of which have been about how to operate the house. I've also been given an instruction manual, which weighs more than a Bible, all about how to make my house function so that I can actually live in it. The day I closed on the house, I was expecting a set of keys. I am clearly from the Dark Ages, because what I got instead was a PDF containing a list of computer codes. The system, it seems, not only controls getting in and out of the house but also just about every other thing you could possibly need to do when you live inside it. After spending several hours just trying to figure out how to enter my own house without alerting the police, turning the coffee maker on, making all the toilets flush, blasting the stereo system, awakening the woman inside the computer who informs me I have arrived, dimming the lights, or setting off a thousand other acts in the circus that is my home, I felt frustrated and helpless—and I still couldn't open the front door!

While I am told that being able to open and close the garage door from anywhere in the world is a good thing, at the very least for resale value, I'm left wondering, *Is there any way to give my new house a lobotomy?* If you're wondering why I bought a smart house, it's because I am in fact technologically adept and could never have guessed how complicated it would be to take on this challenge. Imagine if I had gone another level up and bought a "genius house"? What's clear is that I am going to have to spend a lot more of my time trying to figure out or disable the very system that promises to make my life easier. There's now a term for this kind of experience: they call it "technostress," and most of us know it well.

Yesterday, the mother of one of my daughter's friends sent me a series of photographs from an event my daughter had attended. On the same day, I received an e–greeting card from another friend. Both accessing the photographs and opening the e-card required my joining websites and setting up accounts, which would have taken precious minutes out of my day had I chosen to do so. Since I didn't, I never saw the photos or read the card. I did, however, call my friend and thank her for the warm wishes (which is what I'm hoping the card contained).

A little earlier in the week a client called to cancel her session. She was going to be busy figuring out how to get wireless service or any kind of Internet service to the thirty-seventh floor of her apartment building. She was going to be speaking with the high-floor experts that afternoon and could not risk losing the precious appointment. Her entire day and several other days were consumed with becoming an expert on the interface between the Internet and vertical living.

It used to be we could buy a television and within a day actually be watching it—a TV program, that is, not just a black screen. These days, installing a new flat-screen television (or, as it's now called, "an entertainment system") is an event of epic proportions, one that can take weeks to accomplish. First, we have to become an expert in the new entertainment technology, whether it's the television itself or the system that brings the entertainment to the television, whatever has just come on the market. Next, we must investigate and track down a multitude of experts and different specialty services to help us in our efforts get the television wired or not wired into our existing system. And, finally, we have to figure out how or by whom that will all be set up. Another woman I know, who, like me, is sufficiently technologically savvy, told me that when she was finally able to watch a program on her new flat-screen, she felt the same sense of accomplishment as she had when her child finally got into college after months of applications and interviews.

Our lives are flooded with tasks that feel not only complicated for no good reason but also draining and meaningless. An executive recently told me she receives more than a thousand emails per day. If she were to answer all her emails, she would have no time left to do anything else. We spend a lot of our time just clearing the junk, which we're now forced to do in order to discover anything we might actually care about. Our virtual world has turned into a town dump, a hoarder's paradise, with us humans in charge of picking through the rubbish.

It used to be we that could actually get together with someone or pick up the phone to have a conversation. Then we moved to communicating via email. Now email is too simple, and we need a corporate site through which to send that email. All of these systems within systems steal our time and bury us in clutter, with ever more instructions to digest, things to remember, passwords to record, sites to navigate—just in order to be able to complete the simplest of tasks.

Many people I know now lament that they are too busy to get together in the flesh because there's just not enough time. We are a society besieged by the paradigm of *not enough time*. But perhaps if we didn't have to waste so much time trying to figure out how to get to a place from which we can finally communicate, we might have a whole lot more time—to communicate.

I thought technology was supposed to make our lives easier. But I, and most of the people I ask, feel enslaved and burdened by all the chores and responsibilities that accompany technology. Consider the basic fact that in addition to the tasks technology adds to our lives, we have the task of simply keeping our technology running.

Last week my email caught a bad bug and was out of service for days. Apparently, my email was sending very bad messages to a lot of people I don't know and giving its virus to those who dared open my correspondence. The process of figuring out what was going on and then returning my computer to health took upward of a dozen hours of my time, a dozen hours of my husband's time, and more than one hundred dollars in fees to a computer expert whose services I must now maintain as a part of my business. The month before, it was my husband's system that was hacked, and it meant that he lost a huge amount of information he needed to keep his business running.

In addition to time and money, there is also a cost in terms of anxiety and agitation that comes from being hacked by strangers (or bots) in a strange and virtual world. Feeling violated by an unknowable, ethereal source, we then have to spend our time correcting a problem that is untraceable, seems to exist only in the ether, and has nothing to do with who we are. The fact is malware is everywhere; it is simply an unavoidable part of our digital world. This means that a portion of our time must be allocated to undoing random bad things that come in through cyberspace. Using the technology that is supposed to make our life easier in fact requires an enormous amount of hard work.

For most people, it is anxiety inducing and downright insurmountable to figure out and complete all of the technological tasks that basic living now requires. Yesterday, attempting to obtain, complete, and submit a health insurance form online ate up my entire afternoon. Still, we are under the belief that we have no choice but to toe the line and live this way. The combination of *must* complete the virtual tasks (which are not virtual) and *can't* complete the tasks (not to mention also having a life) feels disempowering and frustrating. If life were a banquet, we would have to serve the computer before we could feed ourselves!

So what are we to do when everything we do requires a thousand other things to do? The question is best answered by another question: *How do we want to live our lives?* If we stay awake to the demands, mindful of what we are giving up, conscious of the way such a system makes us feel, we can indeed make choices and live freely within the system. While it appears that we need to do everything that the technological warden asks of us inmates, in fact, we do not. In truth, we are not prisoners; we have committed no crime. We can reclaim our freedom by saying no to the tasks that demand more of our attention than we are willing to give.

In the digital age, navigating technology has replaced what in another time was the act of going to the well to get water or lighting a fire to stay warm. At this point in history, engaging with technology to complete some of our basic life tasks is necessary and in some ways also helpful. However, the issues are: *Am I living with technology in a manner that is healthy and in balance for me? Is my relationship with technology one that I am defining for myself? Is it conducive to what makes me feel well overall?* As we ponder these questions, it is important to remind ourselves (for we often forget) that we are not the slaves to technology that we often believe we are.

It is still up to us to make choices about what we want to add to our lives and whether we even want to buy into the notion that our lives need adding to. One of the hidden but damaging consequences of technology is precisely the thought that we need to keep up with every possibility that technology presents in order to stay relevant and be part of life. We must become aware of that thought too and not just believe and react to it blindly. The fact that we are breathing and conscious means that we are already part of life—with or without Google. Being part of life is our inalienable right.

Will we be left behind if we don't keep up with every new "opportunity" that technology gives rise to and, in its new role as authority, dangles before our eyes? This is the great fear that is now drizzled into our cultural Kool-Aid. In truth, what we miss out on when we say no to navigating another site or learning a new technology is generally nothing more than the opportunity to understand that new technology, for a minute, until it is replaced by an even newer technology. What we gain, however, by saying no or simply, "Not right now" is profound. When we decide for ourselves how we want to conduct our lives on the basis of what is actually important to us, we discover that we can *be* in our lives instead of just barely keeping up with the life that technology offers. What we gain when we say no to serving technology before and indeed in lieu of ourselves is ownership of our own lives.

If we don't want to give our lives away to navigating technology, then we need to take an active role in our own well-being and investigate our truths and assumptions about the place of technology in our lives. To start, ask yourself, *What kind of time am I spending on technology, and how is that time actually impacting me? What do I believe to be true about my use of technology, which may in fact not be true?* In essence, we need to proactively design our own relationship with technology. It is not a simple task by any means. Trying to live with technology in moderation when we are required to use it for much of our lives presents an enormous challenge. We can't simply choose to power off indefinitely—and wouldn't necessarily want to. But with more awareness of our needs and experiences and more willingness to prioritize our well-being, we can conduct a technological relationship and allocate our time in a way that serves us. If we choose to be empowered, to mindfully make use of technology when it is necessary and helpful and to make conscious choices about when we don't want to interact with it, this is the path to freedom in technology. It is also our best option, given that freedom *from* technology is no longer a realistic choice.

3

can't stop checking

check email more often than I want to and certainly more often than I need to. Scary as it is to admit, I once walked by my own children at the end of a workday, offering them just a quick nod on my way to get to my email, and it wasn't as if I was expecting a note from the president. I am not alone in this. For me, this experience, both acted out and witnessed by me, was a turning point. I suddenly woke up, perhaps by grace or some other force, and was in touch with what's most important to me, my deepest longing, which is not email but loving relationships with my children and other human beings. Perhaps it was a subtle expression in my daughter's clear blue (and confused) eyes that awakened my deeper wisdom. But whatever force of love and awareness startled me into a larger consciousness, I am deeply grateful for its assistance. Thankfully, I was listening. In that moment, I dropped out of my mind, which wanted to connect to the Internet, and reconnected with my heart, which wanted to connect with my children.

I realized that my behavior was not okay with me. I wasn't comfortable with whom I had become around technology. I was disappointed in how I was allowing my mind to turn my computer into a priority above my own children, placing my screen before what was happening in my actual here and now. My deeper wisdom woke me up and told me that I did not agree with what my conditioned mind was telling me was important.

Although I awakened to my real truth in that moment, I still sometimes relapse in my behavior around technology. The difference now is that when it happens, my unconsciousness is short-lived; I wake up much more quickly than before, feeling clearer and more resolved to live in a way that serves my deeper truth. And I do less judging of myself, too, as I also recognize that wanting to go unconscious and distract myself is a natural part of the human condition, one for which technology is a great enabler. If I get involved with judging myself, I just add another layer to the real problem and stall the process of waking up. For most of us, awareness doesn't happen in one fell swoop. We wake up a little bit at a time, a moment here and there, with naps in between. We keep waking up until we are awake most of the time and finally even able to be aware of when we are not aware.

Many people, however, have not yet achieved awareness around technology. The average person now spends thirteen hours per week checking and interacting with email. Given the amount of real-life pleasure that email actually delivers, it seems that the urge to check it is disproportionally high and fundamentally out of sync with reality and common sense.

Most of the emails I receive are junk and go straight into the trash. Some are reminders of tasks that I need to address or events and opportunities that I should know about (and buy tickets for) but don't really want to know about. And the smallest percentage, a few here and there, are notes from friends, family, or colleagues, messages that I am actually happy to receive. It took a while for me to see the glaring disconnect between my real experience of email and my relentless desire to check it, and when I finally did see, I had to I wonder, *Why do we check email so often, and what are we really hoping to find in these little electronic Post-its?*

Email triggers "lottery brain." It's the part of the brain that produces the thought, the hope, the belief that miracles happen, and specifically in our inboxes. To some degree, lottery brain is an adaptive part of us, as it inspires hope, possibility, and sometimes even a sense of agency. When I ask people what they are secretly hoping to find in their email, what the lottery-winning email would be, the replies run the gamut:

> "An old sweetheart, the one who got away, saying that
>   they need to see me."

"A family member [or friend] finally apologizing for
   something they did."
"News that a windfall of money is owed me."
"A perfect job [or professional offer] from someone who
   happened to discover me."
"An acknowledgment of a piece of work [or good deed]
   that I did."
"A note expressing my importance in someone's life."
"A love letter from my partner."
"A note of gratitude [or an expression of love] from
   my child."

There were other hopes, but most fell into one of these general categories.

The fact that it doesn't make sense—our checking something every five to ten minutes that has never or rarely provided the result we are hoping for—is irrelevant. It doesn't need to make sense. In fact, its non-sense-making nature is part of its seduction. Miracles don't make sense, and still they happen. Don't they?

If we were rats in a cage whose food slid down the chute only when we opened an email that made us feel better, would we keep checking, or would we move on to another task that delivered food more efficiently? Probably we would move on and start banging our paws or flitting our rat whiskers on some other surface. We keep checking, not because we derive great pleasure from email, but because in many cases we are addicted. We are not making wise or thoughtful decisions but rather are following a kind of primal urge, which has trumped the part of the mind that can thoughtfully discern whether to check or not to check.

Every addiction, no matter its lure, pulls us out of the present moment—and technology is no different. Technology addiction is no less deserving of our attention than addiction to drugs, alcohol, food, sex, or any other substance or behavior. We can't stop doing something that no longer nourishes us and that very often we don't even want to keep doing. Knowing that we can always check, we become more distracted and more dependent upon something external to escape whatever we don't want to feel or do. Some people start to abandon other, more important parts of their lives in order to engage more fully in their addiction. What's certain is that the more we check, the more enslaved we become.

The next time you feel the urge to check, try asking yourself the following questions (before checking): *What would be the ideal email I could receive right now? What experience would such an email offer me?* Pause for a full two minutes, paying close attention to what happens in your body and mind. Notice if your desire to check changes in any way. In this way, rather than disappearing into addiction, you can use your email cravings to become more self-aware and present.

4

technoholics:
a generation of addicts

Someone recently asked me if I thought that our children's reliance on technology would cause them to become substance abusers in the future—that is, are we breeding a new generation of addicts? Technology does change how we feel. I have experienced this personally, observed it consistently, and had it reported to me by countless people across cultures. Technology provides a shot of energy, a hit of relief, a boost in mood, which makes me and others suspect that it may also be accompanied by a chemical change in the body, specifically one that evokes pleasure. And indeed there is evidence to suggest that engaging with social media triggers the hormone oxytocin, which is associated with feelings of trust, security, and well-being, and may also lower stress hormones.[1] As well, a Harvard study found that the chemical dopamine is triggered in the brain when we use social media for self-disclosure.[2] The fact that our children are constantly getting a fix from their devices may indeed lead them to rely on other substances to stay high in the way that technology gets them high.

And so it makes me wonder. I wonder if the constant use of technology is disrupting or resetting their brains' pleasure baselines to an elevated level. And I wonder if later on they will need antianxiety substances to bring them down from their technological high and calm their jangled nervous systems. And if both of these things are the case, then I would say, yes, this younger generation's reliance on technology may in fact lead to abuse of other substances.

Still, any predictions about future substance use are just conjecture. We don't have to worry about whether our children *will* become future addicts because our children and our adults *are* addicts right now. In a study titled "The World Unplugged Project" at the International Center for Media and the Public Agenda at the University of Maryland, investigators found that "a clear majority" of students in the ten countries studied experienced distress when trying to go without their devices for twenty-four hours. More than half the students failed to stay off their personal technology for the full day. As Susan Moeller, the professor who led the study, explained, the students reported "how scary it was and how addicted they were. They expected the frustration [but not] the psychological effects, to be lonely, to be panicked, the anxiety, literally heart palpitations." They described their phones as physically and emotionally comforting.[3] In another study, it was found that social networking sites are the number one aspect of modern life that people struggle to quit. Twitter and Facebook were labeled as more addictive than smoking or alcohol.[4]

Colin, a recent "camper" at Camp Grounded, a digital detox facility for technology-addicted adults, put it this way: "There's an elevator in my office building, and I realized one day that the twenty seconds it takes for the elevator to come pick me up had become unbearable. I had to reach for my phone; I couldn't just stand there thinking thoughts anymore."[5] There are a lot of Colins out there, and most are not yet seeking help for their addiction. Recent research on millennials (those born between the late 1980s and the early 2000s), a generation that has grown up with technology and is used to having 24/7 access to it, revealed that half of them would rather give up their sense of smell than a critical device like their smartphone and that they'd rather have access to their devices during the workday than a larger paycheck.[6] In another study, it was reported that the first thing 80 percent of people ages eighteen to forty-four do when they wake up in the morning is check their phone. And for 79 percent of this population, their phone is with them twenty-two hours of the day.[7] Technology is the drug of the virtual world—we are already hooked, a society of technoholics.

According to the American Society of Addiction Medicine, addiction is characterized by the inability to abstain from a substance, by impairment in behavior, by sensations of craving, by diminished awareness of significant problems with one's behaviors and interpersonal relationships, and by dysfunctional emotional responses.[8]

Are you a technoholic? Ask yourself the following questions:

- Is your reliance on technology increasing?

- Do you experience withdrawal symptoms when not able to use it?

- Are you continuing to use technology despite knowing that it's causing impairment in your work, health, social, and/or family life?

- Is your life increasingly revolving around technology?

- Have you given up activities you used to enjoy to be able to use technology instead?

- Are you lying about the extent of your Internet usage?

I recently witnessed a man who had forgotten his smartphone charger dashing around the office like someone with a bee allergy who had found himself in the middle of a hornet's nest without his EpiPen. It is not an overstatement to say that we become frantic when we lose track of our personal devices. When told to get off their devices, teenagers can behave similarly to the way cocaine addicts react when you take away their cocaine: agitated, depressed, nervous, volatile, furiously craving the drug, and enraged for being denied it. Another woman I know felt so lost and anxious when she accidentally left her phone at home that after five hours of painstakingly doing without it, she finally broke down and took a cab home just to check her email. Even though she wasn't expecting anything in particular, she admitted that she couldn't stand the agitation that came with not knowing who had contacted her and what she might be missing.

My tween daughter recently returned from a big technology day with a friend whose parents set no screen limits. Upon arriving home, she shared that she felt "edgy," like "something was missing," and that she wished she could sometimes have playdates that were tech free. I was so glad that she could notice her feelings as something out of the ordinary and that she could tell me how she felt. But I also felt fear for the day when "edgy" and "something missing" would be not out of the ordinary, but rather her basic state and therefore no longer deserving of any particular mention or care or even notice.

Many people report feeling the way my daughter does after ingesting too much technology. At the end of a day of excessive tech use, they feel restless and emptied out, depleted and even more bored, as if they have totally wasted their time. And yet, amazingly, most people wake up and do it all over again the next day, renewing the search for something that will satisfy them.

One of my clients sleeps with her BlackBerry and checks it every time she wakes up, all throughout the night. She knows that it costs her valuable sleep time and that it disrupts the sleep she does get in between checking. But she doesn't stop. Adults I know personally and others I interviewed for this book actually sleep with their devices under the covers, even though they are aware that it causes them to feel less rested.

So, too, I (and other moms I know) have had to fire babysitters because they were constantly on their devices when caring for our children. In all of these cases, the babysitters were warned what would happen, but still they continued. At the end of the day, they were willing to lose their jobs to get their fix.

A friend recently told me that she had spent her entire Sunday Facebooking, YouTubing, and tinkering on the Internet. She never went out, even though it was a lovely day, and she didn't interact with anyone directly in the world. She connected with the Internet at the expense of her other interests, which are slowly disappearing. This is becoming a common way to spend a day, the societal norm, not the exception. Like my friend, many children now resist going to the park because they would prefer to stay home and interact with their devices.

Loss of sleep, loss of income, loss of interests, loss of equanimity, loss of life (texting while driving is now the leading cause of death among teen drivers, taking 3,000 lives per year and causing 300,000 injuries), and still we go on using.[9] No matter what we experience or have to give up, most of us still don't view technology the way we view other addictive substances. We know that drugs can cure us when used as medicine and kill us when used improperly, but most of us don't yet recognize that the same is true with technology. Technology can help us when used correctly, and it can also kill us when used unwisely. While the death from technology is not a literal death to our bodies (except in the case of texting and driving), it is a death in our awareness. We can still walk around, but we are not truly alive.

It doesn't happen often these days, but every once in a while someone forgets to bring their smartphone with them for the day or loses it, and they suddenly find themselves alone, vulnerable, with just their own smarts to occupy their attention. After they go through the initial withdrawal and even fear of not having their device, some people actually report a sense of relief and even delight at not being reachable. They enjoy being freed from having to respond to every text and email. "It's like finally getting to be where I am without having to worry about what else is going on," they say. "Without my phone, I don't have to be as externally focused or in a state of perpetual anticipation of what will present itself."

The palpable peacefulness that can result from being unplugged has now become the basis for an entire travel industry. We will go far and wide and pay huge fees to put ourselves in places that force us off the grid. Some of the most expensive destinations on the globe charge us for the opportunity to live temporarily in a world without technology. It seems some of us will pay anything to be protected from our own impulses. These destinations are not unlike rehabs, but without the therapy that perhaps they should offer. And yet, once again, when we get back to the mainland and our devices, fresh with the feeling of relief from not having had them, we plug right back in! We have the self-awareness to know that we need to get off the drug, but the addiction keeps us from making the choices that would honor this awareness.

A recent study found that the average person spends approximately twelve hours per day looking at a screen, with digital media being the most ingested form. The computer occupies more than five hours of our day, with mobile devices coming in second at more than two hours per day.[10] (When I ask young people about time spent on just their mobile devices, a good number report as many as eight hours per day.) And the numbers are rising quickly: it's reported that a child born in 2013 will have spent a year of her life in front of a screen by the age of seven.[11]

"So what?" you might say. "So we play with technology too much? It's not like we're drunks stumbling in gutters. We can still function in the world." The problem with addiction is that it always escalates. We keep needing more and more of our substance—in this case, technology—to stay okay. I have witnessed people giving up many of the formerly meaningful elements of their lives—socializing, volunteer work, cultural activities—in service to their technology addiction. At the same time, addiction causes our self-awareness, our consciousness, to diminish. We use our substance to avoid feelings that are uncomfortable and as a result become less able to manage discomfort of any kind without numbing out or distracting ourselves. Furthermore, addiction causes us to become reliant on something outside ourselves for our fundamental well-being, which in turn makes us feel vulnerable and disempowered. Addiction causes us to regress emotionally and spiritually. It shrinks our lives and us with it, even when the substance is something that has the capacity to expand life.

If we feel better when we use less, why are we using more? And most importantly, why are we not asking this question of ourselves? We may not be falling down drunk at noon or chasing a bag of crack down a dark alley, but we are addicts nonetheless—and technology may prove to be a more dangerous drug than any we've previously known.

We need to take an active role with our technology use and not become a society of addicts raising addicts. It is important to be able to control our use of technology, to be able to use the cell phone when we want to call a friend but not to *have* to check the phone while we're in the shower to avoid missing a text. At the most basic level, addiction just plain feels bad. It stunts us socially, intellectually, emotionally, and spiritually. Addiction leads to unhappiness when the substance starts failing to provide the relief it once did—which eventually it always does.

5

when escaping the moment
is the new moment

For as long as humans have been on the planet, they have invented methods to escape the moment, devising all sorts of behaviors to check out and disappear from now. It seems we are wired to get out of experiences that we don't want to be in. To some degree, it is an adaptive behavior: we move away from what feels bad and could potentially hurt us. And yet, some avoidant behaviors are not good for us and do not serve our growth or happiness. While they allow us to escape from what might feel momentarily uncomfortable, such behaviors keep us limited and stuck in habitual patterns that impede our greater well-being.

Anything can be used as an escape from what we don't want to feel. Alcohol, food, work, fantasy, shopping, television, sex, books, exercise—the exit routes are as limitless as our imagination. But some exit doors are less obvious. One woman I know hides in words. She never stops speaking and therefore never allows the space for any real contact or intimacy with the person she is talking to. Her lack of true connection provides her with a way out of the anxiety that she feels when she is with another person. Conversely, another man spends every moment with friends. While he identifies with being profoundly social, he has also found a way to escape what feels dangerous—namely, his own company. He creates a social self so that he never has to experience his own solitude. We often use socially acceptable behaviors such as these as a way of avoiding what we find internally unbearable.

What's different now, in the age of technology, is profound and profoundly alarming: our method for escaping the present moment is shared, societal, and considered a reasonable way of living. The new way out of now is accepted as the *new now* and not a way out of anything. Being on technology all the time is the new norm.

In the past, the person who was drinking excessively or habitually bingeing on ice cream to escape what they didn't want to feel would most likely know that they were doing something harmful to themself, something they should address. Similarly, while someone who is avoiding their family by working endless hours at the office might not be aware of their avoidant behavior, chances are that those around them probably will notice. Our escape strategies generally tend to fall outside the norms of acceptable societal behavior and thus incite some awareness that what we are doing is abnormal, not good for us, and in need of our attention.

What happens, then, when the normal state becomes the using state? What do we do when not being here is the new here? How can we address the issue when the addiction counselors are themselves addicts? This is the reality we are creating with technology. As a society, we've all drunk the Kool-Aid. We are all checked out, with a new, culturally agreed upon method for escaping now.

Part of the problem is that we do not believe we are using technology as an escape. We do this by singing technology's praises. How can anything that offers so many learning opportunities and connects us with so many other people be considered a method of escape? And yet, as is true with all addictions, such praise is also a justification so that we can continue using. Behaviors can be mindful or addictive. A glass of wine is a delight to our senses; a bottle of it makes us vomit. Books are an adventure and an education, but they become a flight out of here when we use them to hide from the people in our house. Sex can be used to create love, intimacy, and pleasure, but it serves different purposes when we are getting into bed with our fourth stranger of the week. Technology can be used for positive functions, and many exist, but we are also, and with increasing frequency, using it as we would any other addictive behavior or substance—to get away from what we don't want to feel or what we fear we might experience. In a cultural collusion, we lie to ourselves and one another, agreeing that this is not how we are using technology. We are a society in denial, digitally drunk, and as a result we are unable or unwilling to look at the truth of our own behavior with our new drug of choice.

Out of all the escape strategies, all the anesthetizing agents that humanity has invented over time, technology may prove to be the most difficult one from which to wake up.

To break free from our addictive use of technology, we must first realize and acknowledge to ourselves that we are using it as a means to escape the present moment and using it without awareness. The way addicts use their drugs of choice is the way we *normal* folks use technology. While our denial story is convincing for those under the influence—that we can function well, go to work, conduct relationships, and do all the things regular people do—in truth, we are not functioning at the level we think we are when we are chronically multitasking, and we are not taking care of our relationships with the care that we tell ourselves we are. Although our drug comes with sleek and sparkly packaging, shiny Genius Bars filled with other users to hang out with, and, most importantly, membership in the "normal" club, still, like all other substances, our drug will destroy our awareness and render us unconscious.

So what can we do to recover? How can we become free and in control of our relationship with technology? How can we make conscious choices about how we use it and include it in our lives?

First, we need to be willing to acknowledge that something is not working in our relationship with technology.

Then we need to notice and personally take responsibility for our use of technology. The awareness of our craving to escape the moment is not a sociological concept to ponder, not a cultural study to consider, not about what "them addicts out there should do." Rather, awareness is a practice that we actively initiate by paying attention to how we are interacting with technology from moment to moment, starting now. We can do this only if we are willing to look honestly at our personal behavior and the consequences that stem from it.

Self-awareness requires mindfulness, that is, the ability to pay attention without judgment to whatever is arising in our experience right now. Mindfulness is a skill we need to develop—one that we cannot omit from our digital wheelhouse. We can start practicing mindfulness by simply noticing the impulse to get on technology whenever it arises and use that awareness to become conscious of our desire to escape the moment. We can then pause in this desire to use. We can learn to tolerate the feelings of craving, staying conscious and still, allowing it without reacting and without giving in to what our mind is telling us to do to satisfy it: *Click on that app. It will help me feel better!* We can experience the desire to click, check, play, text, wiki, Facebook, Instagram, YouTube, you name it, but without actually doing anything about it. We tune in to what the mind is whispering (or perhaps shouting) at us even as we remain still, without assuming that the mind's suggestions and demands are in our best interest. We examine whether *we*—that is, the larger awareness in us that knows how technology can make us feel—in fact agree with this aspect of mind and want to follow its direction.

The next time you want to use, ask yourself: *Can I refrain? If I don't use, what then will I have to feel?* In the moment of wanting to use, ask yourself: *What is happening right here, right now, inside me and outside me? What's arising that makes me want to distract myself?* Notice what comes in response to these questions, in feelings, words, and behavior.

We can use our desire to get on technology as a red flag, a signal to expand our awareness and investigate *here* and what's uncomfortable more deeply, rather than impulsively running to *there*. We drop into now when we notice the impulse to be somewhere else. Rather than reacting, we take interest in the feeling of craving itself.

The next time you feel the urge to check your device, kindly inquire: *What experience am I now searching for? What happens if I let everything be exactly the way it is right now?*

We can use our feelings of craving to get to know ourselves better, instead of using them to disappear into unconsciousness. Armed with awareness, we are empowered to make decisions about how we want to respond to our cravings, as opposed to reactively obeying their dictates. We remain awake even in the heat of addiction's fire.

So freedom from our tech addiction happens in four simple steps:

1. Being willing to investigate our human (not just our computer) drives. Ask yourself: *Am I willing?*

2. Noticing that we're behaving in a way that we don't like or that doesn't make us feel good. Ask yourself: *Am I willing to honestly look at my behavior?*

3. Making the choice to do something different, to change our behavior. Ask yourself: *Am I willing to change my behavior?*

4. Practicing the new behavior until it becomes habit—and then continuing to practice! Ask yourself: *Am I willing to practice a new way of behaving, which may be uncomfortable, until it becomes habit?*

We all have the inherent ability to tolerate the feelings that arise when we refrain from giving in to our impulses, cravings, and habits, even if we haven't practiced this ability. Human beings have the amazing capacity to consider and even carry out an action that is in complete contradiction to what they desire in the moment. We can choose to say no to that which some part of us believes will make us feel better. We can act from a place of higher wisdom, because another, more discerning, more evolved part of us knows that such a thing will not make things better and that freedom is actually what we want.

We humans possess impulses of addiction and desire, but in truth, we are the masters of such impulses. If, however, the masters are busy texting while walking, driving, conversing, and negotiating the world, they will be slaves to their more primitive drives and behave accordingly.

In the end, the liberation, peace, power, and confidence that come from breaking free from any addiction feels so much better than anything technology could ever offer us. It is profoundly empowering to know that we can trust ourselves, control our own behavior, and thus ultimately take care of ourselves. It is in our power to award the reins to our true master—our deeper wisdom, integrity, and intelligence. Whether we exercise this power will determine what kinds of lives we live within this digital world.

6

information for its own sake

have a friend whose nickname is "Wikiman," because of his incredible love for and attachment to Wikipedia. Wikipedia itself now includes a tongue-in-cheek entry for the term *Wikipediholic*, which is described as "someone who suffers from Wikipediholism," an obsession or addiction to Wikipedia. It also lists a number of symptoms by which to determine whether you suffer from this condition, for example: "If so much as one thing you don't know comes across your mind, you bolt for the nearest computer to see if Wikipedia has a page on it. If it does, you drop whatever you were doing before the urge took hold of you and edit the page obsessively, whether you know the topic or not."[1] There's humor to it, but also truth.

My friend, a most certain Wikipediholic, spends every free moment learning about new things—whatever interests him at the moment. He is on a perpetual hunt for more information. He is also always telling everyone else what he just learned. If you pass a peanut factory on the road, you will hear everything you never wanted to know about the history of peanut production. My friend is a self-made walking book of knowledge. Unfortunately, since he met Wikipedia and the Internet in general, I no longer feel like I get to be *with* my friend, not really. It's as if the information he has amassed prevents me from being able to make any genuine contact with him. He has built a shield of knowledge around himself that keeps me and everyone else from getting close.

Another friend's husband spends all of his free time researching and watching informational videos on his digital device. When he speaks with his wife, he always wants to share what he's learned and show her the videos he's just watched. She complains that she would rather have a conversation with him, one that is personal and not about facts, no matter how interesting those facts might be. She wants to be with him in the present moment, where something fresh can happen, as opposed to receiving facts that are already known. She wants desperately to relate as they used to do and not merely engage in a transmittal of information. My friend feels lonely and neglected in the marriage, as if the relationship itself has turned into a dead fact. As she experiences it, her husband has disappeared into his information technology, his emotional life and their emotional life together usurped by his rapidly expanding intellectual knowledge. Her husband's mistress is the information he spends all of his time with, to which he offers his undivided attention.

Throughout time, people have been trying to disconnect from one another and avoid intimacy. The vast number of addictions and people who are addicted are evidence of this truth. While intimacy and connection have the potential to create joy, they can also feel difficult when our comfortable separateness is threatened. Try looking into another person's eyes for more than a few seconds without saying anything, really landing in the same moment with him. As much as we crave intimacy, being truly together—and not filling the space with content or distraction—can feel awkward and even scary. Being present with another human being can make us feel vulnerable, anxious, and overly exposed. It's not how we're used to relating. Connection and intimacy, first and foremost, require our full presence. To be truly intimate with another person, we have to be able to be intimate with ourselves, to stay with our own experience. For many people, being with themselves is not something they have been taught or know how to experience, and given the fear attached, it's not a skill they particularly want to learn.

The drive to check out, to be anywhere but here, is not new to the digital age, and certainly not something Wikipedia created. What is new, however, is that the availability of information that technology makes possible now offers us a way to achieve our more primitive proclivities with less difficulty and judgment. Gathering information, regardless of its purpose, is now considered a useful and impressive pursuit. Technology doesn't create our avoidant drives, but it does grease the wheels so we can easily satisfy them.

On a recent Jeep tour through the dunes of a remote location, I listened as a man spouted off all the things you could ever not want to know about the Jeep we were riding in. I don't know if he even noticed any of the dunes we were actually on. What struck me most strongly, however, was not his endless stream of information but rather how the other three people in the vehicle were listening intently to his monologue. The other passengers didn't seem to find it in any way odd that this man was going on about the history and science of tires, pummeling us with the reasons why this vehicle could withstand the terrain, filling every moment of potential space with his factual knowledge, all while we were driving through the most spectacular and mysterious natural environment imaginable. The dichotomy between what I was witnessing inside the Jeep and outside it was breathtaking.

There have always been information junkies and people who pride themselves on being walking books of knowledge. But in the digital age, with information so readily available and the *Drudge Report* the new online bible, we bow to information as the supreme deity. Where we were previously inclined to acquire information as a means to another end, to be used to do or create something else, now information is an end unto itself, and looking things up in Wikipedia has become a way of life.

Information is not just an end unto itself these days; it's also a valuable badge. Whoever amasses the biggest pile of information is considered smart and important. Our information accrual is something we are proud of and something out of which we build an identity, as in the case of my friend Wikiman. Furthermore, information is viewed as something that we are supposed to care about, regardless of whether it benefits our lives or we are actually interested in its contents.

But when did it become normal to spend our free time acquiring facts for the sole purpose of acquiring more facts? When did the amassing of information as a goal, without context or implication, become not only normal but also something deserving of respect? Our reverence for information (evidenced by our having named the time we live in the "Information Age"), coupled with the ease with which it can now be acquired, has created a new societal condition: the information syndrome. More and more, I see people in my practice and personal life hiding behind information, disappearing into it as they would with any other addiction, and using it as a way to avoid intimacy with others as well as themselves. Information has become a new defense mechanism. Feeling safe and protected behind our wall of facts, we rebuild the wall daily, only to become ever more unreachable and unknowable. We know a lot about a lot of other things, but we do not know ourselves or one another. Consequently, our internal and subjective world is evaporating into the virtual ether.

As the stockholders of information, we remain an arm's length away from life, always talking *about* it, but never quite being *in* it. Knowing about the tires on which we are riding has become more important than experiencing the ride itself. Life conducted this way becomes an indirect experience. Our intellectual knowledge is celebrated, regardless of whether it's being used for anything generative, and this in turn perpetuates and intensifies the information syndrome. We are effectively sanctioned to keep using information as a hiding place, encouraged to stay information rich but life poor.

If you watch political talk shows these days, the dialogue, if you can call it that, usually involves two people with different sets of facts shouting at each other and not really listening to the point of view the other person is presenting. We share facts, but we have stopped dialoguing. Before information became a commodity on the Internet, its primary purpose was to be an agent of change. We heard a piece of information that did not fit into our already constructed model of the world, and as a result, we adjusted and transformed our model—and we changed along with it. Information had the power to change who we are.

Psychologist Jean Piaget called the process "accommodation," when we have to change or adjust our existing ideas about what is true on the basis of new information we have received from the world.[2] Accommodation is a healthy and important part of human development and evolution. Information syndrome, on the other hand, solidifies what we already believe, ensuring our "rightness" and thus making growth less likely or possible. Accommodation is no longer necessary in the information age. There is enough information for everyone to be "right" and maintain a barricaded system so that we don't have to encounter disruption or contradiction to our existing schema. Technology allows us to instantly find the facts that support what we already believe. While in the past we may have subscribed to particular newspapers or magazines that leaned in the direction of our opinions, still, we could not avoid being exposed to a variety of different ideas. The opportunities to come across information we don't agree with are now diminished. We can easily expose ourselves only to the information that supports our views, stated as facts right there on the Internet. We show up at the table armed with our already decided upon personal truths, and when the information coming *at* us doesn't fit what we already *know*, we stop listening and discard it. The more information we have, the more "right" we are—and the less related. When information becomes an equal opportunity weapon, there is no open room to build consensus and no possibility for something new to emerge.

Just as we carry a drive to avoid connection and presence, so too most human beings contain the drive to solidify themselves and prove that they exist as valuable, real, and unchanging entities. We are in a constant struggle to firm up who we are and what we know and to make that identity and knowing reliable. In truth, we fight desperately against our true nature, namely, impermanence and changeability. Human beings, at least in our more primitive aspects, don't want to have to consider new ideas or modify themselves, because change is frequently uncomfortable and scary. Change puts us in touch with our own ephemeral nature. We opt to be solid rather than fluid, right rather than related or even happy.

Once again, neither technology nor information gave birth to this drive for solidity in the human being. At some point—perhaps when we were evolving from the ocean, from being everything to being a single-cell, seemingly separate organism—our reptilian brain linked this edged and definable separate self with survival. We believe we need our separate self-identity in order to exist. We humans fear the ever-changing, un-pin-down-able nature of what we actually are, and the easy availability of information that technology makes possible allows us to feed our reptilian instincts. Rather than using the vast information now available as a means to become more porous and flexible, to open up our beliefs and identities, many of us are using information as a means to become more separate, isolated, and protected from the world.

If we are interested in truly educating ourselves and growing internally, not just swelling up with more facts, the skill that's required is a different kind of listening. When we use information to create an emotional barricade or to cement a position and identity, we are listening defensively, with the purpose of protecting ourselves from anything that is not like us. Listening becomes a way to make sure that we have been recognized as the keeper of "right" information. So, too, we listen to determine whether any new information coming back at us will endanger our position and thus our identity as the one who is "right." We state our facts and then batten down the hatches to make sure nothing gets through that might cause us to have to investigate what we know we know.

To break free from the information syndrome, we need to change how we view the exchange of information: to realize it is a dialogue with the potential for growth and not a battleground with the potential for annihilation. We can do this in part by loosening our identification with what we know and what we believe about what we know. When our identity as a smart or knowledgeable person is no longer dependent upon our information being accepted as right, we are free to enjoy information without our self-image being threatened. At the same time, when our identity as a valuable human doesn't rely upon our being the owner of information, we can relax the whole process of sharing and receiving it. At the end of any exchange, our identity (and existence) can remain intact, regardless of how our information is received.

We break free from the information syndrome when we allow ourselves to:

- Gather information as if curiosity itself were doing the gathering

- Share information as if we were a mouth floating in space

- Listen to feedback as if we were ears floating in space

In order for information to be an agent of positive change and growth, we need to be able to approach it through fresh and unencumbered eyes. We need to snip the cords that bind information to our sense of self. Without these two elements distorting our view, we can meet, understand, and share the vast quantity of information that is now available in a way that benefits all of us.

In addition, we can change our relationship with information by learning to accept contradiction as a necessary and healthy part of communication. If we understand that another person's differing information and opinions can coexist with our information and opinions, without either of our personhoods being destroyed by the contradiction, then we can genuinely listen to and relax with what another knows and believes. When contradiction is not seen as something that has to be resolved in favor of one side or the other, then we can open up our ears to what we are hearing and be porous without feeling endangered. Listening with the confidence that contradiction is not dangerous, that differing truths can coexist, creates a space in which the exchange of information can once again be a positive and forward-moving event.

In truth, we do not need to treat information as if it were a weapon. We have done that *to* information, turned it into that, by using it to define ourselves defensively. But information itself is neutral. We can reestablish a friendly and respectful relationship with information now—appropriately in this Information Age—so that we can enjoy it, grow from it, and exchange it peacefully, as we would any other resource, without ever having to own it or be identified with it.

Furthermore, we can liberate ourselves from the information syndrome by simply paying attention to how we feel as we gather, share, and offer information. Do we feel closer to those with whom we are sharing, as if we are connecting and building a bridge through the information? Or do we feel more separate and isolated inside our information bubble? Start paying attention to your relationship with information. The next time you set out to share what you know, ask yourself:

- Am I present and available to what is being expressed within this exchange of information?

- Am I trying to get through this communication without being destroyed as a person, trying to survive with my already established beliefs still intact?

- Am I in a dialogue, or am I trying to win a battle for rightness?

- Am I genuinely listening in the exchange of information, or am I scanning for holes in the other's information to solidify my own correctness?

In such an inquiry, the body is a wonderful keeper of clues. Ask yourself:

- What is the state of my shoulders, neck, jaw, and abdomen?

- Is my body tense and tight as I participate in this exchange of information, as if it were in some kind of competition for survival?

- Is my body relaxed and breathing deeply as I share facts and listen to feedback and the information that others also know?

- Is my body shut down, without an awareness of the sensations being received?

This style of physical inquiry will raise our awareness about our relationship with information and help us uncover the moments when we have stopped using information as a path to fluidity, growth, and change. Ultimately, becoming aware of our own behavior and motivation is the first and most important step in opening up to the larger process of change.

7

an epidemic of boredom

The movie previews had not yet begun, and the midfifties man in front of me was playing with an app on his phone. It's not just kids these days who are spending large parts of their days playing games on their devices. According to an Internet study, 53 percent of all adults now play games online (81 percent of those between eighteen and twenty-nine), with one in five playing every day or almost every day. The average young person will rack up 10,000 hours of gaming before he reaches age twenty-one.[1] That's about the same amount of time he will spend in the classroom for all of middle school and high school. We are gaming with intensity, striving to avoid the frightening plague of our time—boredom. In the digital age, boredom is a danger that is always stalking us in the shadows. In an effort to stave it off, every free moment must be filled up with some form of entertainment—a game that leads nowhere, creates nothing, and may be only mildly engaging, yet that has the power to keep boredom at bay.

Even our technology itself is now falling victim to the threat of boredom, as we are increasingly in need of companion technologies to supplement our primary source of distraction. It is not uncommon to see people now interacting with a multitude of screens at the same time, while also tweeting and texting out commentary about what's happening on their screens. It appears that just one form of distraction is no longer enough to fend off the biggest risk: that of being with ourselves.

It is common now to hear adults use the word "boring" when referring to unentertained time, time when they don't have something to occupy their attention, and to label themselves in that unoccupied state as "stranded" or "stuck." To be with just ourselves is boring, and boring time is time to be killed. While I have always heard such complaints from children (my own included), our increasing reliance on technology has turned chronic boredom into an adult epidemic.

The verb *to bore* means "to hollow out a tube or make a hole in." In the digital age, we view empty space as nothingness, as death. But what if open time and space could be experienced as a womb fertile with possibility, awaiting impregnation? In truth, open time *is* the mother of invention, the opportunity to birth something new. Could we rediscover the delight in having time to ourselves and not knowing what might unfold? I wonder what effects our dread of boredom and of our boring selves are going to have on us as a society? What are we breeding into and out of the human species through our unwillingness to welcome the possibilities offered by not having something to do?

It's in between activities and tasks that we give life to unformulated intuitions and reignite the embers that linger within us. Nothing to do is the most nutrient-rich food for the human imagination. It's in the unfilled spaces that we develop the confidence that comes from being able to engage our own minds and know that we can take care of ourselves in this way—without needing a suitcase full of devices to babysit us. This kind of confidence is profound and lasting, not at all the same as the feeling that comes from knowing that we have enough apps and enough bars on our phone to stave off any potential boredom. All of us, children and adults, need to be able to tolerate and reside in the experience of having nothing to do—it is part of growing up, as well as part of just being alive. A hollow is a place where a nest can be built.

When we send our children to their rooms to play on their own, we are giving them the opportunity to discover and invent something, to engage themselves. Playing alone—without a device—teaches children that they can rely on their own creativity and imagination. Furthermore, it allows them to experience what it feels like to imagine something into being. Such play makes children self-reliant and teaches them to take ownership of and responsibility for their own attention.

According to child-development expert Nancy Carlsson-Paige, author of *Taking Back Childhood*, "Kids need firsthand engagement—they need to manipulate objects physically, engage all their senses, and move and interact with the three-dimensional world. This is what maximizes their learning and brain development. A lot of the time children spend with screens takes time away from the activities we know they need for optimal growth."[2]

With modern-day adults as role models and technology as their new virtual playground, children are losing the instinct and ability to imagine and create on their own. In addition, as Carlsson-Paige points out: "the activity itself, and how to do it, is already prescribed by a programmer. What the child does is play according to someone else's rules and design. This is profoundly different from a child having an original idea to make or do something."[3]

For the first time in fifty years, researchers are finding a significant decline in creativity among children, particularly young children from kindergarten through sixth grade. This decline is believed to be caused, at least in part, by the drop in play that has accompanied the rise of technology in children's lives.[4]

I see this in my own home as well as in the homes of my friends: children are comfortable imagining and creating *in response* to something on a device. But without the device there to prompt them and set up a structure and options, these same children are at a loss. It appears that as a result of their interaction with technology, children are becoming reactive rather than proactive; they are becoming passengers rather than drivers in their own engagement.

As a three-year-old, my daughter used to love to be in her room and play alone with her dolls and other toys. Listening at the door, we would delight in her most delicious sounds and stories. She was within a whole world of play, a life that she had created and to which she loved to return. Soon after she met her first smartphone, however, she started begging for it, throwing tantrums for it. She would start the day by making the sliding gesture with her pointer finger, which on the device moves the screen forward. Imaginative play, time with herself in her room, quickly became less interesting and sometimes was even experienced as a punishment rather than an opportunity.

Having now witnessed the dramatic effect the smartphone has on her willingness to play by herself, I am in the process of taking the device away as a potential form of distraction and entertainment. Every day I allow her to play for a little less time, which means that I have to say no a few more times per hour, or minute. Weaning her causes tantrums, and the whole process is quite hideous and very loud, a bit like stabbing myself in the eye with a serrated knife and then doing it again a few minutes later and then again a few minutes after that. But I know (and hold onto the knowing) that my saying no is important for her well-being, even though it can feel excruciating in the moment. Getting kids off technology is not for the faint of heart, not once they've tasted the relief and glee that a princess video on YouTube can provide. Getting off technology is, in fact, hard for the whole family. In the end, for me, it's a matter of using my resilience and my ability to stay present and connected with my love for my daughter, my deeper wisdom, and my clear intention to teach my child to enjoy herself without external entertainment. I want her to know her own internal resources and to trust the imagination and intelligence she contains. Thankfully, the more I say no, the more she returns to playing on her own, engaging herself, and being happy and proud about it.

When it comes to engaging ourselves, there is an aspect of us that is wired to opt for the passive route. Human beings like to be entertained, and we like it when things come without effort. Ultimately, however, we need the ability to imagine and create, to be able to engage ourselves—not simply distract ourselves—in order to be self-sufficient and feel fully alive. Without this ability, we will become robots, relinquishing the best of our humanness as we accomplish tasks and frantically fill up the spaces between them with distractions. So, too, we will lose the great joy to be had when we create something out of nothing—and the knowledge that we are fundamentally okay with only our own imagination to play with, the capacity to know ourselves as not boring.

Can we rescue our relationship with unfilled time, wrestle our respect for its importance back from the growing flocks of Angry Birds? We can, but it's a choice that we must make consciously. In so doing, we must be willing to face the boredom itself, to experience the agitation and restlessness that appear when we stop gaming our way through life.

We need to decide we will face the fear and anxiety that show up when we put down our devices, and we will stop running away from this naked now. Instead of getting better at outrunning boredom, we can get better at noticing when it appears and using it to become more conscious and present. Rather than immediately medicating boredom, we can leverage it as a great opportunity to meet ourselves.

When you find yourself reaching for your phone as you stand in line at the grocery store or playing with an app when you are in between tasks, ask yourself:

- What would I have to feel if I couldn't play with my device right now?

- What experience is here now when I resist the urge to distract myself?

- What are the sensations in my body that I am labeling as "boredom"?

- Who inside is noticing that I am bored, and who makes the effort to fill it?

- What happens if I allow the boredom to be here?

We can investigate, with curiosity, the experience that boredom is, without having to turn it into something dangerous. So, finally, ask yourself: *Is the experience of investigating boredom boring?*

By taking this approach, we can stop squandering the most fertile ground we possess, stop wasting the incredible energy that is our own attention, stop collapsing into the habits of avoidance with which technology so powerfully tempts us, and stop believing the thoughts that tell us unfilled time is nothing, nowhere, and of no inherent value. A space unfilled is *not* nothing. Rather, it is no thing and simultaneously no thing *yet*—neither of which is nothing. While it may seem like just a benign indulgence—a game of Drop7 during the previews, a round of Tetris at the bus stop, and maybe a few Fuzzle hits before bed—time filling in this way has insidious effects on who we are. Indeed, it is our very abilities to create something out of no thing, to be with ourselves, and to know (and take confidence in) our own imaginative intelligence that are now at risk of being lost.

8

when technology bosses us around

The restaurant listed a grilled chicken salad on its entrée menu. I was craving a green salad (the same thing as the grilled chicken salad, but without the chicken). I asked the twenty-something waitress if the chef could make the simple green salad instead. She said that she would have to find out, but she doubted it. "You have the lettuce, tomatoes, and cucumbers?" I asked. She nodded. "You have the bowl?" She nodded again. But then she informed me that there was no button on the computer corresponding to my request, and therefore I couldn't have the plain salad. She said, however, that I could pay for the grilled chicken salad and pick off the chicken—that was the best the computer would allow.

"So the computer will allow me to pay $18.95 for a simple green salad?" I inquired, keeping my voice calm. "Which, by the way, would be the same price I would pay to have the full meal. And then I will have the added pleasure of picking off the chicken?"

"Precisely," she said, smiling and moving away from the table. "Let me know what you decide," she called back with an odd lilt of cheer.

Although we humans create computers, we have forgotten that these machines are our tools—and not the other way around. We are now deferring to technology as if it can choose the answers for us rather than help us choose our own. Do we need to create a program that will remind the computer—or, perhaps more effectively, us—who the boss is here?

Decision-making and self-reliance are just as vital to our personal development as they were when Ralph Waldo Emerson wrote his famous essay on the topic in 1841. It may have been more than one hundred and fifty years ago, but all these years later, his words apply even more starkly: "A man should learn to detect and watch that gleam of light which flashes across his mind from within, more than the luster of the firmament of bards and sages."[1] How do we prevent ourselves from becoming a society of conformists, blindly accepting the information provided by a ghost inside a machine? How do we avoid turning our authority over to the computer, allowing it to determine what we can and cannot do and, most importantly, what we actually want? As my young daughter often asks, "Who made you the boss of me?"

To be self-reliant is to know and trust that we have the answers for ourselves, that our intuition and intelligence are the source of our greatness, and that we can be trusted to create and guide our own destinies. Thinking out of the box may not be the path of least resistance, but the path of least resistance may end up being the path of extinction and will undoubtedly be the end of our awareness. In fact, we need some resistance in our lives to stay awake and not slip into unconsciousness. If we humans do not want to end up as sleepwalking passengers in our own lives, then we need to examine our willingness to turn our lives over to technology, to relinquish the right to determine our fates, and to allow the finite box of the computer to stand in for our infinite wisdom.

9

our phones are getting smarter,
but are we?

An unknown writer (often misattributed as Albert Einstein) eerily prophesized: "I fear the day that technology will surpass our human interaction. We will have a generation of idiots."[1] Is today that day? As we cede more and more responsibility to our devices, are we surrendering our human intelligence? Are we forgetting how to think?

Exhibit A. I was at the home of a friend, an educated and highly intelligent person. A serviceman was working in the house at the time. Upon completing his work, he handed my friend a bill. On it he had written, "2 Plumbing Services: $295." The following exchange then transpired.

> My friend: "If you remember, you told me that you
> would charge me your lower rate of $130 for the
> first service and the higher rate, $165, for the
> second. I think you may have charged me the higher
> rate for both."
> Serviceman: "I remember our conversation. That's why
> I charged you $295."
> My friend: "But you didn't itemize the jobs, so I don't
> know if that's the case."

At this point my friend went to fetch her bag from the other room, searched through a variety of coat pockets, finally tracked down her iPhone (a process that took several minutes), and then began tapping on her screen (which took another minute or two). A screen calculator then appeared, more tapping transpired, and in an instant there it was: "295" in neon green.

My friend had made the choice to put all that effort into searching for her phone and typing in the information—all to avoid doing the work that actual thinking would have involved.

Exhibit B. This is an exchange I overheard at the AT&T store.

> Clerk: "I will need your phone number to upgrade
> your plan."
> Customer: "Hmm. Well, I never call myself, so I don't
> know my number." She then turns on her smart-
> phone to retrieve her phone number.

Ideally, we should delegate responsibility for irrelevant tasks to free ourselves to do more meaningful work. But in the case of technology, we are turning over relevant tasks—math and memory, to name just two—to free ourselves to do what? Get to a higher level of Angry Birds? Play more Words with Friends? We are choosing to surrender the tasks of living to technology, but instead of becoming higher functioning creatures, we are becoming, to some degree, more helpless. There is evidence to suggest that we now make more mistakes in our tasks because we assume the computer will do it for us—until it doesn't. When things go wrong and the computer fails, we don't know what to do to correct the problem. The more we choose to use our computers to figure things out, the less we are able to figure them out for ourselves.[2]

Are we abdicating the process of thinking? Do we no longer consider it our responsibility to think things through for ourselves? And yet abdicating the thinking process is not a real option. Processing experiences, making connections, generating new ideas . . . these require the skills of invention, creation, and progress, the skills that separate us from less evolved species. But more than just distinguishing us from our four-legged friends, thinking is important because of what it offers and what it means at a deeper level.

Thinking, the kind that makes use of the mind as the incredible tool that it is, is profoundly life enhancing and nourishing; this ability is one of the great fortunes of being born human and having a brain. Thinking can be incredibly joyful, exciting, and empowering. Once again, it is up to us to decide which skills we are willing to give up and which we want to keep in our wheelhouse. Just because the computer says it can think for us while we check out and eat a box of donuts doesn't mean that we have to check out and eat the donuts. We are not anesthetized; we still have the power to make conscious decisions. If we want to continue to be able to think skillfully and want thinking to remain a part of our life experience, then we must consciously resist the temptation to turn it over. We must own it, practice it, and claim it as our human right and delight.

What is certain is that we cannot cede our thinking to technology and still expect to be very good thinkers. Indeed, if we forget how to think, we may not be able to figure out how to think again.

We are conditioned to believe that easier means better, that the less we have to do, the happier we will be. But often this is not in line with people's actual experiences. We feel good when we are productive and engaged, which requires effort. Being able to store and retrieve information from our phones frees us up not to have to remember anything. And yet having to remember keeps our minds strong and gives us a sense of mastery, mental acuity, and continuity. When we are able to pull up things from the recesses of our minds, dig deep into the memory files, it feels good. We feel alive, fully functioning, sharp. We get to experience the particular sensation that is the brain turning its wheels, working. On the other hand, losing our memory, which happens when we cede memory to our devices, feels disempowering, disabling, and even frightening.

While it is easier to store phone numbers in our smartphone than to remember them ourselves, a client in her late twenties recently confessed that it makes her sad when she doesn't know the numbers or addresses of her friends and thereby loses an element of intimacy in the relationship. As she put it, "It's as if I don't know my friends that well anymore." There is a reason that we call remembering something "knowing it by heart"! This same client told me that she used to love being able to surprise her buddies from elementary school by remembering their street addresses from childhood or the first phone numbers they had while growing up. She experiences not knowing her newer friends' private information as a great loss. Memory is more than just a list of facts; it is part of the very fabric that creates closeness and meaning in our lives. Memory is a part of what makes us who we are.

As technology makes more and more things possible and does more for us in everyday life, we have to make choices about what we want to use among all of these possibilities. When we turn something over to the computer, there is a good chance we will lose the ability to do it ourselves and thus become ever more dependent on technology for basic living. Knowing that, what responsibilities are we willing to surrender? Is it okay that the computer will know how to do something but we won't? Are the many seemingly small choices we make to abdicate responsibility leading us down a highway to helplessness?

We need to stay awake as we hand over these tasks and not allow ourselves to become impotent because it's easier than keeping aware. Because we can does not mean that we should, want to, or must surrender our abilities. We can say no to the easy route simply because we decide that being able to do things ourselves is still important, valuable, and meaningful. We can say no because we actually want to keep making the effort, sometimes even when it is not pleasurable. What is more effortful is often the stronger and more rewarding option. What is desirable in the short term is often not what feeds us in the long term. It is important that we ask ourselves and contemplate these questions at a deep level:

- What experiences nourish me?

- What qualities do I value within myself?

- What are the actions that create such experiences and strengthen such qualities—even if I also find them challenging or time-consuming?

- And, finally, what aspects of life feel meaningful, even if technology has made them no longer necessary?

In truth, what we decide to relinquish and what we decide to keep are up to us.

PART
2

our relationship
with others

10

your friend or your phone?

One of my clients is separating from her husband because he cannot separate from his smartphone. These days, when couples go out to eat together, the first thing they do is pull out their devices—if they're not already holding them—and place them on the table between themselves and their partner. There is nothing stranger than watching two lovers in a dark and quiet restaurant, drinking wine, feeding each other treats, while simultaneously watching every few minutes or so for the lights and buzz of their devices to go off. Even stranger is when one of them actually puts down their glass, unravels a foot from their partner's calf, and pulls away to check that lit-up device. Maybe to find out that a Groupon for a pair of sneakers has just become available?

There are no more tables for two. Tables for four now accommodate our most intimate encounters: two humans and two devices. In the digital age, it is normal not to give any one person our full attention. When we are together, even in our closest relationships, it's often the case that a part of us is not present, as we are subtly (and not so subtly) awaiting the next alert from our devices. The person in front of us is not enough, at least not enough to warrant our turning away from what else is possible, the what else that our smartphone constantly beckons us with.

If you haven't been in solitary confinement over the last ten years, you've probably had the experience of sitting down to a meal with a friend and watching them pull out their smartphone and place it on the table. You know what it feels like. When our phone or our partner's phone is with us, it's part of the meeting, and its presence changes the interaction. In a recent set of studies by Andrew K. Przybylski and Netta Weinstein of the University of Essex, they discovered that simply having a phone nearby, even if it isn't checked, can be detrimental to our attempts at interpersonal connection. When a cell phone was within reach, people experienced a lowered quality and closeness in their relationships. They also had a harder time feeling trust and reported that their partners showed less empathy.[1] With our devices present, we can't fully settle into what is happening here and now in the human relationship because some part of our consciousness is distracted, in relationship with our electronic device and a potential other. Even when the chime is not answered, often we still pick up the phone, check to see what the chime is about, place the phone back on the table, and then return our attention to the person we're actually with. This whole process interrupts the experience that is happening with the other person. It requires a reentry into the conversation, and that person, who is now returned *to,* feels less important because their company is not deserving of our exclusive attention.

What people do with this message of less importance is determined by their psychology. Some try to be more interesting, to make themselves so worthy the other will turn off their device. Others retreat into insecurity and loneliness. Still others just get on their own device to navigate their way out of the present moment and away from the relationship; in this way, the disconnection and invalidation process is balanced. As a psychotherapist, I witness the myriad ways we are changing psychologically as we generate new defense mechanisms to manage the devaluation we experience in the face of such behavior. We downgrade the importance of our human friends when we award equal or higher status to our technological companions.

Attention is how we show each other we matter. The gaze of someone who is really *with* us, not distracted, not elsewhere, but here, is like a gift of the most divine substance. There is a flow of energy, an energetic circle, that occurs when two people are wholly with each other, undistracted, fully present. In this circle, it is possible for both individual "I's" to disappear; it is possible to discover a third entity, which is the relationship itself, without separation. When we include our devices in our interactions, we disrupt the energetic circle of intimacy and, with it, the possibility for two "I's" to become one "we."

As a society we have lost the distinction between public and private space. It used to be that if you were at home with your family or out on a date or some other such personal encounter, you were not available to everyone else. The setting aside of times and places where the outside world was not allowed, special places just for the special people in our lives, added to the sense of importance of those relationships. Now, always powered on and available to the public through our devices, always relating with the public through social media, many of us have stopped granting a special importance to those in our private world. The public is now as important as the private.

If we still want private space to feel different from public space, intimate relationships to feel different from nonintimate relationships, then it is up to us to separate the two and treat them differently. We need to have times and places where we are not available to everyone but only to those who really matter to us. The choice to deem certain people and places worth turning off the "who or what else?" button for infuses those people and places with meaning. A relationship delivers what we put into it. If we treat someone as important, they become important. If we treat them as no more important than any business associate or acquaintance, they will assume that generic value in our life. Our behavior determines the depth of our relationships and, with that, the amount of nourishment we receive from them.

The next time you go out with or stay home with someone you care about, turn the smartphone off, turn the tablet off, turn it all off—better yet, put the devices away, out of sight. Make the conscious decision to create private time that is different from public time. Take the risk that for the two hours you will be at the restaurant you won't need to be reached. Decide that whoever is calling can wait a few minutes for your attention, in service to the relationship now present. Ask yourself, *Is what I am checking for on my device really as important as this person?* This system of just being in one place with one other person worked for eons—before technology made it something strange, before it became something that we need to consciously choose, before it required going against the social norm. The small act of simply refraining from putting your phone on the table—dare I even suggest leaving it off altogether—has the power to improve our lives in ways that are immeasurable.

11

asking for the attention
we still need

Technology is now our competition, the mistress that steals the attention we need. It is what our friends and loved ones are talking about, gazing at, and paying attention to—in place of us. We are creating a relationship with technology that takes away something we need, one another's undivided attention, and in so doing, we are left feeling vulnerable. Paradoxically, by choosing to ignore others in favor of our devices, we indulge our laziness and self-involvement while we simultaneously exacerbate our loneliness.

With technology's presence now solidified in our lives, we need new rules for our relationships with other humans. And, perhaps most importantly, we need to be able to ask for a certain kind of undistracted attention from those we are close to—or used to be close to before we all started prioritizing our devices.

Most everyone finds it difficult to allow the vulnerability that comes from exposing the parts of ourselves that we may consider unsavory or unlovable. It can be very scary to ask for what we really want and to communicate how we really feel, especially if it's not the way we think we should feel. To admit that we sometimes need to be at the center of someone else's attention, not just a sidebar to their screen or to the dozen conversations they are conducting through their device, is an act of great courage. When we ask a friend or partner for what we really need, we take a risk. We risk learning that our friend or partner might not want or be able to give us what we need. We expose our hearts. We show our true selves, rather than the "acceptable" version we believe is lovable. When we remove the armor from around our hearts, we risk getting hurt, being judged for our needs, and feeling shame. Most of all, we risk rejection and feeling unloved. The need to be loved, to belong, is at the very core of our wiring; it is our most primal requirement for safety. Thus, allowing ourselves to be vulnerable is no small affair. Allowing ourselves to be vulnerable is a real threat to precisely what we believe we need to be okay.

When our priority shifts from keeping a friendship going by controlling our circumstances to actually uncovering and living from how we actually feel, that's when something genuine can bloom. When we are honest about what we need, the response we get forces us to look at the truth of the friendship, its limits as well as its limitlessness. Our truth beckons the larger truth of the relationship into the light. From there, we can mindfully decide which friendships we want to continue investing in and to what degree. The illusion of a friendship is not the same thing as a friendship, no matter how we try to fill in the holes.

In asking for what we really need, we not only give ourselves the chance to receive the care we long for, we also deepen and sanctify the relationship. We set an example and standard of truth that the friendship can then rise to. I suggest we step up and be brave: take the risk that comes from telling the truth. Ask a friend or your partner to put away their device if that is what you need; tell them what would make you feel more connected and cared for. We can be the first to bravely voice what we really require, knowing that deep down it's the same thing everyone really requires. We can be the courageous ones who open the door and offer permission to others. Ask for the best from your friends and intimates, and you will receive the best friends you deserve.

12

last-minute-itis

Ten minutes before we were to meet, a friend texted me that she was canceling because she had not slept well the night before. She wanted a rain check. This was followed by a big "XO" and a frowning emoticon. It was 9 a.m., and I was already at the breakfast spot. Another text I received the same week read, "Running late. Get there soon." This text too was accompanied by an emoticon, only this guy's little yellow face appeared to have a look of frustration, somewhat different and more nuanced than the frown I had received earlier in the week. As it turned out, that "running late" text meant that I would be waiting another half hour until my colleague arrived.

A technological disease is spreading through our society. I call it "last-minute-itis." To find out if you suffer from this condition, consult the following list of its most common symptoms:

- frequently texting friends at the last minute to cancel plans, often after the friend has already reached the scheduled location

- frequently canceling plans with friends because you don't feel like going or something else you would rather do came up

- frequently texting that you are "running late"

- forgetting to show up for scheduled meetings because you didn't "put it in your phone"

- consistently choosing to leave plans "loose" and
  tentative, until a plan is "firmed up," often via text,
  at the last minute

These days, when we make a date to meet someone in person, there is a growing likelihood that the meeting will not actually happen, with most cancellations occurring within an hour before the appointed meeting time. Until our companion actually appears in the flesh (not on FaceTime), we expect our smartphones to light up with either a "can't make it" or at the very least a "be there in 10" message.

Before cell phones and social media became so important in our lives, we were more inclined to honor a date we made with someone, unless something came up that made it truly impossible. We were more prepared to commit to a time and a place in one conversation. Setting the date didn't require another dozen communiqués to firm it up. Furthermore, it was assumed that we would get to the location at the arranged time—that is, on time. Even if later we didn't feel like going, we went anyway because it would be considered rude and disrespectful to cancel at the last minute. I remember when making the choice to carve out a slice of time to spend with another person held a kind of sacredness that we did not violate. Or perhaps we just felt it was important to uphold a certain basic code of manners in our relationships, to do the right thing.

While there's no way to say with scientific proof that people were more civilized or considerate in past decades, what is clear from the reports I receive and all the people I've interviewed on this topic is that the digital age has ushered in a culture of noteworthy bad manners. In addition to my own research, a study by the modern etiquette publisher Debrett's found that three in four people now think manners have been destroyed by cell phones, laptops, tablets, and social media.

It is now standard and acceptable behavior for people to cancel five minutes before they are to arrive, simply because they know they can do so via a text message—without ever having to witness their friend's disappointment or irritation. It is now the exception for people to actually call when canceling. The texting canceler is off the hook, never having to experience a moment of discomfort.

As one friend aptly described, "Not only are emoticon-heavy last-minute cancellations the new normal, there is also an acceptable framework of lateness we now accept as a given in our device-dependent society." Although I am still careful not to act on it, I notice a change in my own attitude, as if I feel a certain slackness about keeping plans now that I can slip out of them with such ease. I can remember a presmartphone time when being late was seen as a form of wasting someone else's time, which was inherently not okay. Because it's now possible to alert our companions that we are going to waste their time, it's become acceptable to show up when it works for us, not necessarily when we said we would. Sometimes I wonder how we used to be able to do it, to drop whatever else was going on in order to honor an agreed-upon meeting time. Somehow, it was just what we did, the civilized choice. Now many of us behave like self-involved addicts or not-yet-evolved adolescents who can't put down our drug of distraction, suspend the pleasure of being on our devices, and turn our focus to getting out the door to meet our commitments.[1]

While it would be another act of laziness to blame our smartphones for our own bad behavior, it's still true that technology has made bad behavior and laziness far easier for us, and I would even dare say acceptable. By so readily offering us the opportunity to act out of our baser qualities, technology has unwittingly made many of us more self-involved, disrespectful, and undisciplined. It's allowing us to live by our whims and do whatever feels easiest, which is not necessarily what's right or kind or even what sits well with our own moral compasses.

But when we make choices based on "I don't feel like it," we are denying ourselves the opportunity to develop resolve, to push through challenges, and to generate grit—the experiences that build strong character, integrity, and also success. We are allowing technology to foster a society in which it is acceptable to treat other people, their time, and the time we spend with them as insignificant, an afterthought. It's the ultimate casual culture in which everyone and everything is disposable. And, perhaps more disturbingly, we are handing over our power to technology, allowing *it* to steer important ethical choices about how we behave.

If compassion and kindness are aspects of our more evolved selves, and selfishness and laziness belong to our more reptilian selves, then yet again technology is taking us in the wrong direction. Moreover, we are using technology in a way that causes us to lose sight of the sacredness of our relationships. I felt crappy and disposable when my friend canceled on me at the last minute. This kind of behavior makes us feel like we don't matter, not just our time but also our company.

I have to admit that when the time comes to get together with another person, no matter who it is, there is often a part of me that does not feel like going. It's easier to stay home, or I'm tired, or it simply takes less effort not to interact than to interact. But more often than not, after meeting whomever, I find I'm glad I went. Something unexpected and interesting happens, or I remember that I really do like spending time with that person, or just being out in the world. I feel connected, or it feels good to push through my resistance and not succumb to what seemed easiest. I always benefit when I don't trust the part of my mind that tells me it's acceptable to cancel. We mature when we exercise the discipline and discernment that it takes to move beyond our momentary desires. Technology, sadly, is leading us away from choosing such opportunities for growth.

Increasingly, my clients describe being unable to make decisions in their lives or to commit to the decisions they do (sort of) make. This creates a kind of paralysis and a life that feels like it never happens. The ability to make choices is one of the most important life skills we can develop. With the cell phone now making it acceptable to avoid having to make firm choices, we are losing this critical life skill. What I consistently witness in my practice is young people who are perpetually on the fence between choices, inert and paralyzed by the open-endedness that our culture of technology creates and supports. One woman who had a particularly difficult time making choices described her life as one of moving widgets from one side of her desk to the other and then later moving them back.

People talk frequently about not being able to choose between their options, in part because choosing involves accepting the losses that accompany all choices. We get to have what comes with *this* choice but have to give up what comes with *that* choice. Technology creates a society that believes we shouldn't have to give anything up. It's understandable that we don't want to do without, but we no longer believe that we're supposed to. Unfortunately, being unwilling to give anything up makes decisions impossible.

Our use of technology both creates and intensifies our inability to commit. The fact that it is acceptable to bail in the final hour is evidence that we no longer see commitment as an important and necessary part of life, one that not only builds character but also actually helps us create a life in which we shape the things that happen. Instead, we live in a constant state of "we'll see." Unfortunately, in order to feel grounded, we need to write some of our dates in pen, not pencil. If you want proof of this, answer a child's question with "we'll see" and watch as they immediately become agitated.

The next time you make a plan with someone, notice what it feels like to *commit* to the plan inside yourself—to the person, place, and precise time. Shut the proverbial back door that the cell phone opens. Set an intention to build grit. And then notice:

- By removing the possibility of a last-minute texted cancellation, by closing your options rather than keeping them open, do you feel more spacious and relaxed?

- Does closing the gates to other options allow you to be more present and attentive to where you are now?

- Do you feel more connected or warmer toward the person you'll be meeting because you made the commitment to see them and spend time with them?

- Do you enjoy the anticipation of looking forward to something that you've decided is going to happen?

- Do you feel more dignified as a result of committing to do something and giving someone your word?

Paradoxically, leaving ourselves endlessly available results in our being unavailable to others and to life. When you close the door to what else there is, then what actually *is* becomes valuable.

13

swimming in the shallows

For many people, their primary form of communicating these days is via text. Short bits and blobs of life, quips and banter, and sometimes just emojis and no words at all are what pass for communication. Whatever snippets we send out into the ether, the recipient experiences the communication alone. We don't see the face or hear the voice of the person receiving our text, which also means we don't have to experience the impact of our words. Texting is easy, controllable, and safe.

As already discussed, we are wired to seek ease and comfort, to find the path of least resistance preferable to the one that requires effort or discomfort. Technology is the path of least resistance when it comes to communication. It's easier to break up with someone via email than to do it in person, easier to text someone about your hurt feelings than to tell them face to face, easier to use technology to make a demand than to ask for it in person.

Relating to other human beings in real time and face to face takes effort and energy, focus and presence. There are moments when neither person has anything to say. These gaps are a shared experience and a part of the communication itself, as important as the words that fill the spaces and often more powerful in their connective value. Still, silence can feel awkward, and real-life relating almost always includes an element of awkwardness. So, too, difficult emotions can arise in real-life exchanges. There are moments when things can get bumpy and painful with another person. Misunderstandings happen, hard truths are revealed, and feelings can get hurt. Real relationships are not for the faint of heart.

As texting, Facebook, Twitter, Instagram, and other social media have become our primary modes of communication, it seems that we are losing our ability to tolerate discomfort and challenge in our relationships, to stay present and work through the hard aspects of being in relation to other human beings. A disturbing trend has started to pop up in my office and also in my personal life. People are coming and going, in and out of friendships and romantic relationships, with a new level of ease and frequency. Charlie, a thirty-something client, treats romantic relationships like gaming apps on his phone. As he sees it, there is always a new game on its way down the pike, an unlimited array of options for something better, and thus he doesn't need to struggle with difficulty. If a person becomes dull or presents a problem, he can and even should simply delete them from his life and move on.

Jane, another woman I knew, got used to the ease, lightness, and controllability of her communication on Facebook and other social media. As a result, she acknowledged that when difficulty or conflict arose within a real relationship, rather than confronting the issue and addressing what was happening, more and more often she would find herself dropping out of the whole messy affair. Increasingly, too many of us are choosing to disappear from (or text our way out of) the challenges that all relationships include. We're simply not addressing that which is hard to address. Our use of technology is creating a society in which human relationships are becoming less worthy of investment or effort than before. It makes me wonder if we are truly losing the ability and the willingness to muddle through the harder parts of life.

When we address a conflict with another person, the process is often messy and tough. Conflict is not easy to handle. It is not something we can control or package; how the interaction will unfold, come together, or disintegrate is unknowable. I don't think there ever was a time when we liked to experience conflict or feel difficult emotions. But we used to accept difficult feelings, discomfort, awkwardness, and challenge as a part of life and relationship. We used to understand that if we wanted to have anything good, there was going to be an element of hard work involved. We no longer seem to believe that discomfort or challenge is an inherent, unavoidable, and also important part of being in relationship.

It appears that we are attempting to eliminate the parts of relationship that don't fit into our new 140-character culture.

The reason we are willing to address conflict with a friend, to go through that challenge, is because we care about the friendship. It matters to us. So we agree to wade through that muddy river to get to the other side, where the friendship can be restored. In psychology, we call this process "rupture and repair." The bond that is formed after wading through the conflict together is actually stronger than it was before the conflict happened. When difficulty is confronted, it strengthens what was there before the difficulty. Given our increasing unwillingness to struggle through conflict, even some of the time, in order to save something as important as a friendship, could it be that we are now at risk of not caring about much of anything anymore? Ask yourself: *For what or whom am I willing to leave my comfort zone?*

By no means is this to say that we should stay in relationships no matter what or that the only reason we drop out of relationships is because we are unwilling to face conflict. Some relationships need to end, for many valid and healthy reasons. But more of us are disappearing from relationships the minute some bumps appear in the road, because we don't like bumps. Ask yourself: *Am I using technology to avoid the bumps in my relationships?*

There is an alarming flippancy these days in the way some of us relate to one another, a lack of investment in the meaning of relationship. The result is that we are left with a whole lot of friendship lite, but not much in the way of nourishing and deep connections. Relating and connecting in person take work. To meet a friend for a meal or a walk requires that we show up, not just physically, but with our full attention and internal presence. However, in part as a result of technology, internal presence is something that people are less able or willing to offer and less interested in developing than before. If the choice is working at being present or playing Angry Birds, well . . .

By living through email, social media, and texting, happily within our comfort zones, it's easy to remain inside our private mind caves, hanging on only to the version of ourselves that we like. Going out into the world with people demands that we expose ourselves, risk being affected, risk leaving our mind caves and moving into life. Real connection requires that we loosen our death grip around our fixed ideas of who we are and become willing to open to the flux and flow of life. When connection is controlled through our devices, it is far simpler to avoid being porous, and thus we avoid having to change. By controlling the closeness or distance of our interactions, we eliminate the risk that we will get involved and lose ourselves in the experience of life.

The ease we are wired to seek often translates to shallowness, which is in direct opposition to what most people are truly craving these days. In my practice—and everywhere, in fact—I hear people expressing the need for more depth in their relationships and in general. Our daily lives feel increasingly shallow and irrelevant, and the more our relational lives move into the realm of technology, the more starved we become for profundity and meaning in our interactions. Relationships are a primary source of depth in our lives, of meaning and connection—all the things we're lacking. Depth in our relationships can only develop, however, if we are willing to behave with maturity and discipline, to act in accordance with what really matters.

We will never end up anywhere profoundly satisfying by avoiding difficulty. We need to bring mindfulness to the challenges that relationships present and address them directly and with awareness. Each moment that we are willing to be uncomfortable in a relationship, to live in and through the messiness, is a drop of gold in the relationship itself. Investment in the hard stuff is ultimately what makes relationships worthwhile.

14

a remedy for disconnection

There is no right way to walk through pain. My tendency, when confronted with it, is to spend more time alone. During a recent period of challenge, however, I decided to move through it differently. I needed support, so I reached out to a number of people and shared my struggles. Through the act of sharing, I learned a valuable lesson about relationship in the digital age—not so much via the responses I received, but through what transpired afterward.

In the encounters after the difficult time was over, what I noticed most strongly was the absence of continuity. People had little memory of what I had spoken of just a couple months earlier. When I met with my friends again, often their attention was divided, partially occupied by a device's screen. In defense of this absence of continuity, some might say, "If you weren't in your previously difficult state of mind, your friends probably didn't want to take you back to something upsetting." Others might mistakenly describe this kind of interaction as "very Zen," in that only the present moment exists after all.

But is it possible that we are so overstimulated and overburdened, so stuffed full of information in our new digital world, that we can no longer retain the intimate details of another's life? A recent study by the National Center for Biotechnology Information looked at attention spans—that is, the length of time a person can focus on something without becoming distracted. It was found that in 2000 the average person had an attention span of 12 seconds. In 2015, our attention span had fallen to 8.25 seconds, 1 second less than the attention span of a goldfish.[1]

Regardless of how we explain, understand, or justify it, continuity as a relationship practice may soon disappear. From the reports I get, it appears that this experience of interaction without continuity, a historyless connection, is now quite common. It is also one of the proofs that communication itself is increasingly more suited for computers than humans.

It's interesting that a woman with whom I'm not especially close forced this issue to my attention. I had run into her at our local grocery store on an exceptionally bad day, a day when I really needed support. She asked how I was, and I told her the truth. At the time, she listened, was kind, and offered some helpful guidance. It wasn't what happened in that interaction that struck me so intensely, but rather what happened a month later. When we ran into each other again, she began the conversation with, "Are things any better with your family? Did your husband get that job?" When she asked me those simple but very specific questions, tears filled my eyes. Similarly, I recently started a conversation with a friend by asking how her daughter was feeling, picking up the conversation from where we had left off the previous month (when she had shared that her daughter was depressed). This friend, whom I have known for years, thanked me for remembering that her daughter was going through difficulties and then thanked me again for inquiring about how she was doing.

Are we at risk of becoming so distracted because of our devices that we now thank each other for basic kindnesses, for being human, as if remembering what another person is living through is somehow an extra service and not an integral part of relationship? Continuity is not just the rain that feeds the tree of friendship but includes the very tree itself.

It has always been the nature of phenomena to appear and disappear; what's different now is that there is no longer a place for what was, for history or context. Things appear and disappear with no trace of ever having been. We are less and less interested in history and relate to it as something dead, something that no longer serves a purpose. We have a conversation (often via text), and as quickly as the words appear on our screens, they evaporate into digital space, along with the other person who was there "with" us in the ether. Conversations appear as a form of entertainment: Now you see it; now you don't. Now you know it; now you don't.

It is becoming unnatural for us to hold our friends' lives in our hearts, to walk around carrying those lives as part of us. It's as if that aspect of our character is being conditioned out of us; perhaps we are preparing for a time when our smartphones will take over the heart's job of remembering. It's as if we are always clearing space on our internal hard drives so that nothing remains, not even our most intimate moments. Our human conversations are starting to resemble tweets; they come and go without any of them meaning much of anything, without their providing any glue for the spirit.

Relationships are built and depend upon our retaining a place in one another's lives, a place that is continuous, that does not simply disappear once we power off. Continuity is the essence of human connection, and it is suffering under the distracted consciousness to which we are now succumbing.

The result of this kind of continuityless interaction is loneliness. Without continuity, we feel isolated, like no one is really *in* our lives with us, holding a piece of us even when we are apart. Moreover, continually beginning again and again makes the act of relating exhausting. It becomes our burden to recreate and reinsert ourselves into the relationship we believed already contained us, like having to get a boat out of a windless harbor with each fresh encounter. Most importantly, without continuity, the feeling of being known—the distinguishing feature of friendship—is forsaken. We are known only for what we decide to share on that particular day, and the container for the friendship is discarded after each use, like a plastic wrapper.

If we want to experience more connection in our relationships and in life in general, we must make the effort to listen attentively in our conversations, not multitask while we're "listening," but *listen* with our full attention. When we listen, we remember. In truth, we desperately need to pay attention to one another, to listen closely and remember the specifics of the lives of those around us—to care enough to create a thread line.

The next time you are in a conversation, stop and ask yourself:

- Am I really listening to this person?

- Am I opening to their experience, actually taking in
  what they are sharing?

- Have I fully landed in this conversation, or am I trying
  to get somewhere else?

If you're not really listening, don't judge yourself, but do ask yourself what's in the way:

- Am I formulating my answer while the other person
  is speaking, needing them to hear about me?

- Am I distracted, thinking about something else?

- Do I feel like I don't have enough time to land here
  in the conversation?

The invitation is simply to get to know yourself as a listener, to notice what is true, so that a new way of being present might be born.

Creating continuity is a choice that we make in relationships, one that profoundly transforms not only the lives of those with whom we come in contact but also our own. If we want our relationships to have more weight, to feel more meaningful, we need to infuse them with the depth that paying attention, listening, remembering, and acknowledging what came before will actually engender.

When people are dying, they almost never talk of work, entertainment, or other distractions. They talk about their relationships, about love. If we want to live well as human beings in a digital world, we need to recapture the exquisite and profound skill of listening, of remembering, and of real presence. In other words, we need to remember the most important thing and act from that place.

allow me to help

was entering the gym when I realized that I had my iPhone but had forgotten my headphones, which meant there would be no music during my run. A First World problem, for sure, but nonetheless an annoyance. Weighing whether to return home (a mile away) or to work out to the thumping and agitating computer-generated tunes of the gym, I decided to ask the thirty-something woman at the desk if there were any headphones in the lost and found that I might borrow for an hour. She checked, but there were none. And then she did the thing I haven't been able to stop thinking about: she offered to lend me hers. "I won't need them over the next hour," she said, with a friendliness that felt unfamiliar and even startling. Within a minute, we were walking back to her office so she could fetch her headphones out of her purse. "If I'm not here when you're done, just drop them on my desk," she called to me as she headed back to her post up front.

My strong response to this woman's simple kindness was what tipped me off to the importance of this "anachronistic" event. I found myself thanking her profusely, as if she were offering me a kidney. Should I buy her flowers, an iced latte, a newfangled something? I felt the need to honor her out-of-the-ordinary gesture.

The fact is, as simple as it was, her gesture doesn't happen that often these days. It was a small event, yet it signifies that as technology becomes the center of our attention, people are no longer our main focus.

Now that technology is the mode by which we conduct almost all business and the computer is the centerpiece of work life for most of us, people are being reduced to numbers on a screen, impersonal codes the computer can understand. When an employee makes a decision regarding someone's problem, that employee is generally looking at a screen and not at the face of the person with the problem. Chances are the human assisting will never have to look into the eyes or hear the voice of the human in need. Our relationship is with a computer, not a person. This disconnection between the person of service and the person in need of service makes indifference and unkindness easier and more common.

Technology can be used in this way to detach ourselves from our empathic connection to other human beings—to *not* feel or identify with what others are living. (Most of us have been at the receiving end of this when talking to a corporate "customer service" department.) Staring into our screens, we can easily forget that people are actually human beings, with feelings and lives, and that they are really just like us. When we forget that truth, we stop caring about them.

And then sometimes it is different; someone cares and makes an effort—personally. When they do, it feels beautiful. We remember that we're in this life together and that we can, in fact, choose to help one another. We remember our ability to be of service and the joy of simply helping another person. In such moments, we remember our basic goodness, our inherent kindness, all of which we are at risk of losing touch with when we are only touching technology.

What is so amazing about what the woman at the gym did for me is that she took personal responsibility for a situation. She became personally involved. She thought about what she personally could do to solve the problem that was in front of her. She did not suggest I register with their website to find out more about what to do in the case of no headphones. She did not assume a passive or self-protective attitude of noninvolvement. She did not invoke corporatespeak or reference the company's policy on borrowing headphones. She did not defer my problem to someone else or claim that she did not have the authority to make such decisions. She did not refuse involvement for fear that I would sue her in the event that her headphones got wrapped around my neck and choked me. She did not make me fill out forms or leave a deposit and a blood sample. And, finally, she did not tell me there was nothing she could do. She did none of the things that are considered normal in the digital age. She simply got up out of her chair and went and got her own headphones so I could borrow them.

I found myself feeling protective toward her, worried she would get into trouble for doing what she did. I have even chosen not to mention her name here because of my fear that she might be fired for having broken some corporate rule that forbids employees from getting personally involved in a gym member's life. As crazy as I think it is that she could get into trouble for this simple act, I also realize that it is possible. And, further, my own worries demonstrate how deeply the fear of personal involvement has burrowed itself into and infected our cultural consciousness. The beautiful truth is that this woman saw a person who needed something that she could give, and so she moved from the heart without concern for potential consequences. She did not hold back in order to keep herself safe, but rather put herself out there and likely found a different kind of safety in the act of giving.

It's true that many of us are now actively supporting social media and crowd-funding campaigns for important causes, signing online petitions, and wrapping our Facebook posts in the flag of the country most recently struck by terrorist acts. While these acts of virtual virtue are important and make us feel good, too, they are not the same as being helpful on a personal level, taking action to assist the person right in front of us. Technology is allowing us to be helpful and involved, but from a distance. We get involved without having to risk anything. So, too, often when we're told how we can be helpful virtually, that easy response doesn't support our learning all we really need to know about a situation, so that we can thoughtfully consider how best to help. Virtual virtue can also result in our indifference to appeals for help in the real world, the nonvirtual world, because we think we've already done our part online. Technology makes it easy for us to avoid the personal suffering of those who need our help in our local communities—because we've already clicked on "give," so we're off the hook.

The gym employee's simple, direct, and completely natural action reminded me yet again of what we human beings are really made of, what sits below our modern, fear-soaked conditioning. In the moments when our basic human nature peeks through, it is a profound event, worth paying attention to. Instead of routinely trying to defend ourselves, perhaps we can remember to ask the simplest but most important question of all: "How can I help?"

The truth is we can all make the choice to get involved personally. We cannot avoid using technology in the workplace, but we can cultivate the awareness to remind ourselves that there are real people and lives behind our screens. We can encourage ourselves to remember that the person whose face we can't see, whose voice we can't hear, probably longs for exactly the same things we do, for themselves and those they love. We can consciously decide in our own personal and professional lives to remember our shared humanity and not separate ourselves out so that we can close off our hearts. We can make the choice to come from kindness, which may entail doing things differently from what we see done around us—and that's okay. Kindness isn't always the easiest choice, but it is the one that nourishes our hearts. We can remain connected to our basic humanness, prioritize humanness over technology, and choose not be part of the dehumanization process that technology facilitates. In simple ways, we can remember to listen with our hearts and not just our heads (or digits), and, if given the chance, to look into someone's eyes. In short, we can decide to care. When we invite this aspect of ourselves, our basic goodness and compassion, into our daily lives, it feels beautiful, both for those it touches and for ourselves.

Small acts of direct and personal kindness make a profound difference in our individual lives and the world overall. It is almost always when we are expressing kindness that we feel the deepest happiness, when we remember that we are indeed in this life together with other people, whether we know them or not. We need only remind ourselves that it is in our power to choose how we want to show up as human beings in a technological world.

welcome to the family, smartphone

t's not easy to have children. The fact that it isn't easy does not mean that it isn't glorious—it is. But children need relentless attention and engagement. It isn't always easy to give them what they're asking for. I have a three-year-old, and there are days when getting down on the floor and playing with the soft toys or staging a Barbie fashion show is just not on my bucket list. I do those things sometimes, maybe even often, because I feel I should. An enormous amount of parenting relies on the power of *should*, which arises out of our love and sense of responsibility. *Should* is wired into a parent's brain, probably to insure the survival of the species, and it needs to be, because much of what goes into parenting would not happen if it relied purely on *want*. The *want* that is genuine for most parents is wanting our children to be happy. And yet the things we have to do to make that happen are sometimes things that we simply don't want to do.

Dragging the sled over the six icy blocks to the hill in the park the other day, my hands numb after surrendering my gloves to my child, my feet wet, my back aching, my list of things to do for work overflowing, a truncated conversation with my husband still ringing in my ears, I looked over at the beaming smile of my daughter, her body steaming warm with three-year-old loveliness, and that's when I bowed to the beauty of *should*.

And then there are the times when *should* loses out to *want*, or, perhaps more appropriately, to *don't want*. A few mornings back, I was working on this book. I had no babysitter, my older daughter and husband were out of the house, and I was on deadline. But here at the base of my desk was my doe-eyed three-year-old with a big grin on her face, beckoning me to come and play with her and her dolls. Aargh! I told her that Mommy needed to work this morning, that she could play on the floor, and that I would watch her from my desk, which wasn't exactly honest, because I needed to focus on my work. Still, I encouraged her to play on her own right next to me. No luck. She insisted that I play with her on the floor, which I again declined, lovingly.

This process went on for some time, escalating in intensity, until my daughter became agitated and destructive, scribbling on things that shouldn't be scribbled on and generally creating mayhem. By this time I'd lost about twenty minutes of work time and was getting a bit agitated myself. Even though I wasn't playing with her as she requested, my daughter had managed to kidnap my attention anyway, and thus, play or no play, no work on this book had happened. "There are certain things that grown-ups just have to do," I told her, in a last-ditch effort to stay off the floor and also retain my sanity. Unfortunately, while this platitude came from a loving place, it was a concept my daughter had neither interest in nor capacity to understand. She wanted my hands-on engagement, and she wanted it now.

That was when she saw *it*, my smartphone, gleaming from under some of my papers like a shimmering angel sent to rescue us both. She immediately begged me to watch the videos she knows sit inside my little white toy. "Princess, princess, princess," her wailing went. "Princess it is," I said, and off and away we went. With the life mask of technological anesthesia comfortably in place, she and I both knew we had found a way out of our shared frustration. In that moment I simultaneously felt both relief and disappointment in myself. The smartphone does not create the problem that is the challenge of parenting, but it most definitely provides a way out of some of its problems—at least at a surface level. Sometimes I wonder if my daughter also feels both relief and sadness when she gets what she wants this way, though it's not what she really wanted, which was me. The hard truths are that sometimes who we wish we could be is not who we are and what we wish could happen cannot happen; we have to open our hearts to this truth, too. In such challenging moments, I often remind myself of what psychologist

D. W. Winnicott called "the good enough mother," the parent who does enough but is not perfect, and, in this case, not perfect inside the quagmire of technology.[1] We do the best we can and trust that good enough is good enough.

A few days after the incident in my office, I witnessed a father and young teenage daughter on a lunch date. Although the two were physically sharing a meal together, the father spent most of his time on his smartphone, making calls and playing games. When he did momentarily put his phone down, he kept one eye on it, never taking his hand entirely off the device. The girl, who was technology free, appeared sullen. In between game rounds and conversations with others, when the father did address his daughter with a shred of his attention, she made no eye contact and hardly responded. Her voice was weightless, like the place she seemed to occupy in her father's life.

Technology use is complicated when it comes to children and parents. Sometimes we have to give ourselves permission to surrender and let them or ourselves have the device because, purely and simply, we need a break, a way out of what's happening. Sometimes giving our children the device or using it ourselves is better for everyone when worse things could happen if we have to keep interacting. We parents have to be able to take care of ourselves as well, and if we do only what appears to be best for our children, we won't always be well enough ourselves to be good parents. But at other times, the truth is that we do need to cultivate more awareness and determine whether we are using technology to escape the important and difficult responsibilities that parenting requires.

Technology use is a family problem, not just a child or a parent problem. Almost 70 percent of children think their parents spend too much time on their devices, and a survey by Opinion Matters also revealed that more than one-third of the children they questioned are worried that their parents are incapable of shutting off their devices.[2] Children are losing their parents to technology, just as parents are losing their children to it. We're all disappearing down the same rabbit hole.

Furthermore, technology has become an important tool in family dynamics, a way that we communicate priorities, values, feelings, power, and everything else. Even when our smartphones are on mute, our technology is communicating something to our children. Technology, and specifically how we choose to integrate it into the family structure, is now a significant aspect of child-rearing, one that needs to be considered thoughtfully. When we contemplate what kind of family we want to create, we must take into consideration the role technology will play. We need to learn how to interact with it in a way that serves our family's well-being, whatever "well-being" means to us.

One woman I know said that she gets on her phone when the family is together because her sons want to get on their phones. She's on technology because they're on technology. At a deeper level, though, this is not what our children really want. They want to feel that someone is with them, paying attention to and interested in them. Sometimes we can be that parent, and sometimes we can't, but more importantly, isn't it our job as parents to decide what's best for our children, even when technology tells them that technology is what they want? We need to ask ourselves if we (personally) are raising orphaned children, choosing to allow technology to take over as surrogates for our own attention. Even more importantly, we need to reclaim our role as the real authorities in our children's lives. They are our charges. Technology doesn't decide what's best for our children; we do.

It's also important to become aware of the messages we're sending our children when we consistently stare into our own screens and not their eyes. The old stereotype of the father with his nose buried behind a newspaper usually included a mother who told him to put it down and talk to his kids. But what about now, when both mom and dad are riveted to their devices and there is no one left to be with the children? This is not to suggest that we are doing something inherently bad when we send a text while walking our child home from school, or call a friend from our cell phone when we need to, or any of the regular things we do as people living with technology. We just need to be honest with ourselves and take responsibility for the choices we are making around technology and their potential effects on our children. We want to be mindful of and ultimately okay with the messages we are sending with our own use of technology.

If, however, we consistently, day after day, spend our time interacting with technology, paying more attention to our devices than to our children, then we are indeed communicating some damaging content. First, we are saying, "I am more interested in what's happening on this screen than I am in you." Second, we are saying that texting or playing games and essentially distracting ourselves is a valuable way to spend our short time on this planet. Finally, when we choose our devices over our children (which is how a young mind understands a parent who is always on technology), we are saying, "You, my child, are not important, not worthy of my attention." While there is always the possibility of healing from such experiences in the future, still, we don't want to burden our children with such emotional baggage if we have a choice—which we do.

Children of technology-consumed parents will more than likely end up playing their own games later, if they're not already, not only because they were taught that this is a rewarding way to spend time but also because they won't trust that anyone wants to pay attention to them. When we are staring into our devices, we are not present with our children. Children are sometimes too young to realize that it is we, the grown-ups, who are at fault and instead interpret this experience as the result of their own failing. What they understand is that they are not worthy of our attention. And indeed, this is what we are demonstrating to them when we would rather connect with our smartphones than with them.

Because it's easier to surrender to the anesthesia of technology than it is to do the hard work it takes to engage our kids does not mean that that's the best choice. Because it takes much less work to hand over a device to them than it does to say no over and over again does not mean that we have to. And because our kids may accept our divided, diluted attention and appear to be happy regardless does not mean we can behave this way without consequence. As I've already said, sometimes we have to take the path of least resistance because it's actually what is most wise. But too often our choice to submit to technology is born out of a desire to check out and surrender to what feels good or easy. Such choices are not guided by our higher or conscious selves, and so they're not likely to lead us to a state of peace or well-being. In truth, we can be peaceful even when a three-year-old is howling at us—that is, if we are rooted in our deeper wisdom. To be mindful is to make our choices and conduct our lives in the light of awareness. If we want to take good care of our children, we have to behave consciously and with wise discipline around technology. And when we make the hard choices and decline the path of least resistance, it's important to acknowledge and honor our own backbones and offer ourselves compassion for the difficulty that wise discipline usually includes.

Most of all, we need to cultivate awareness in the family environment and conduct ourselves in a way that is in sync with what we genuinely value, the kind of family we want to create, and the principles we want to impart to our children. When *what is most important* is driving your decision to take the phone away from your child or put it down yourself, the discomfort that such a choice entails becomes far more bearable because it is infused with clarity and the strength of knowing why you are choosing the bumpier path.

As parents, we are awarded a most profound power and privilege: to be able to give our children the experiences of being loved and of knowing they are valuable human beings. This is our task in creating new people. Being present and gifting them with our attention, even in silence, is how this task gets accomplished. There is nothing virtual about love. It is created and enacted through the mindful choices we make, one moment at a time.

The next time you start to put a device in front of your child's nose or your own, pause for a moment and ask yourself:

- If I couldn't use technology right now, what would I have to feel?

- What do I want to have happen here so that I can best take care of my child, my family, and myself?

- What course of action would be in alignment with what is really important to me?

The purpose of asking these questions is not to stop you from using altogether, but rather to invite your larger awareness into your mental dialogue about technology. Whatever decision then comes as a result, whether to use technology or not, allow that choice to be okay.

17

engineering life one
autocorrected letter at a time

The autocorrector changes a letter here and there. "So what?" you might say. The "so what" in this case is that the smartphone's autocorrector is not only reconstructing the words we write, switching one letter or word for another, but is also in the process changing our relationships and redesigning our reality.

The autocorrector, when not itself recorrected, contributes yet another mirror to the funhouse that is human communication. As a psychotherapist, I have (lovingly) come to see most of human communication as some form of projection or transference. That is to say, when two people are conversing, for the most part they are not exactly communicating accurately—that is, neither person is hearing what the other person's words mean to the person saying them. Instead, the listener is hearing what the other person's words mean to the listener, as the words are run through (and are sometimes distorted by) their own complex system of memories, history, thoughts, experiences, and (the biggest one) identity. It used to be that at least the words being distorted in communication were the original words a person intended to use. Now, however, with the addition of the autocorrector, even the original material is distorted, leaving us with a distortion of a distortion.

Consider the following examples.

Case 1. I am in a heated text discussion with a friend. I write, "NO Gail," and hit "send." Without my awareness, the autocorrector texts my friend, "GO Girl." The next communication I receive from her is suddenly chatty, without the rancor of our current disagreement. I look back, notice the smartphone's "correction," and burst into laughter. Ultimately I decide to go with the new, altered reality, noticing how meaningless the rift was and dropping it altogether.

Case 2. I am setting up plans to get together with an acquaintance, and she asks whether I can meet her in downtown Manhattan, or do I need to stay on the Upper West Side? I write back, "UWS" for Upper West Side. Unbeknownst to me, my smartphone replaces "UWS" with "Yes." My friend takes this to mean that yes, I can indeed travel downtown, so she sends me the address of a bar in Greenwich Village. I repeat that I need to stay on the Upper West Side in order to get back to work. The next text I receive is a Freudian analysis of why I was originally willing to go downtown but have now changed my mind. Apparently, I was going to surrender, but then decided to control the experience. Despite my explaining to her that my smartphone's autocorrector had agreed to the downtown location, the interpretation of me has already been voiced. Our relationship changed as a result of those three letters being altered. To this day, I am not sure if she ever did believe that I had originally written "UWS," but it is a moot point. Our relationship now journeys down a "corrected" new path.

Case 3. A therapist receives a suicidal email from a patient. The therapist responds and signs her name, "Patty." Her autocorrector changes her name to "Party." No more needs to be said about this exchange.

Case 4. I text a friend to ask if she can babysit. Although my friend is obese, we don't talk about her weight unless she is telling her tales of her latest diet. She doesn't share her real struggles with me. Nonetheless, her weight is always an unspoken presence in the room. When she responds to my request by saying that she can indeed babysit, I write back, "That's great!" My autocorrector responds with, "Cover rear!" We share a good laugh (she knows I didn't write it), but I sense that it caused her pain by bringing something shameful to the surface in my presence. That autocorrection introduced a new reality in our relationship: speaking loudly of the unspoken. I don't know if she wanted this new element in our relationship, but once again, a moot point. In reorganizing those few letters, the autocorrector reorganized our relational path.

Case 5. Jill goes to meet the father of her boyfriend, Jack, for the first time. An older man, Jack's father has just purchased his first iPhone and is excited with the new toy. The next day, in deference to his technological delight, Jane decides to text him instead of calling. She writes, "Thanks so much for last night!" Unfortunately, her autocorrector sends, "Thanks Douche for last night!" Not fully understanding the autocorrector function, Jack's father is not amused.

Of course it is always possible to proofread our communications before sending them. But have you ever tried to correct the autocorrector? I recently tried to write a word that my autocorrector didn't recognize, and it took me seven attempts to get the word that I wanted onto the screen. The autocorrector is a very persistent editor. Sometimes, even after you correct autocorrect, the device sends out its own version anyway.

But regardless of whether or not we want to spend an extra five minutes on each communication—attempting to correct and correct again what autocorrect rewrites—the fact is that the ghost in the machine has been assigned the task of turning what we mean into what it "thinks" we mean, using an algorithm masterminded by people we don't know and who don't know us. While the autocorrector presents itself as the palace servant, it in fact holds the throne of the digital age. Once a communication has been altered and sent, that communication and all that it impacts can never return to its unaltered state. Though sometimes harmless, the autocorrector is a symbol for a more frightening and potentially dangerous aspect of technology. When we allow our words to be "corrected," we also allow not only our meaning to be "corrected" but also the reality that then transpires from that meaning. Are we comfortable surrendering meaning, reality, and life to an algorithm? If your answer is no, then ask yourself:

- Am I willing to turn my autocorrector off?

- Am I willing to invest a bit of time and effort to ensure that the words that come from me are decided by me and not my device?

- If I'm not willing to turn it off, why not?

If we ourselves are on autopilot with technology, the autocorrector may seem like just another welcome time-saver, but if we consciously consider what we are agreeing to when we agree to let our devices speak for us, we may find that we want to make a different choice.

18

is technology our new savior?

A client described her brain when it's immersed in the online search for love as being like an orange slush—an amorphous mush with sharp, icy edges here and there. She told me that she devotes every free moment she has outside of work to surfing the dating sites, scanning the faces, perusing the profiles, crafting and responding to emails, tinkering with her profile, planning and attending dates, and on and on. She is on a feverish hunt, gazing into the virtual eyes of one online suitor after another, winking and frowning, and all the while asking herself, their image, and the universe: *Could this face—could you—be my future husband?*

Over the years I have worked with countless people who have fallen down the rabbit hole of Internet dating and online friend communities. For some, it has resulted in romance, friendship, and lasting relationships, but for others, nothing came of it. For most, regardless of the outcome, the process itself became obsessive and painful. Hypnotized by the possibilities that these sites seem to offer, they became convinced that the virtual world would deliver what they needed in the real world. The experience is seductive and addictive; it makes it look like there are infinite potential partners and friends to be found. In my client's orange-slushy brain, it appeared that everything she wanted and needed was right there for the taking. All that was required was a bit of effort, though not the effort of changing out of her pajamas or leaving the house.

My client felt empty and anxious when she came to see me on this particular day. She felt as lonely as she had ever felt, despite all the dating and communicating she had been doing over the recent months. I asked her what experience she was really longing for, at the bottom of all the searching. She said she wanted to feel loved and to be chosen as the most important person in someone's life (which she had never been to either of her parents). She wanted to be the destination for big love, and she also craved a place to share her own big love. As she saw it, the virtual world offered the possibility of giving her the life experience she craved, but the lonelier and more deprived she felt, the more real time she invested and the more desperate she grew. As she turned herself over to the Internet, her single-mindedness increased, and she became wholly dependent on the Internet to provide for her. As she understood it, Match.com now held the power to make her feel "chosen"—but it also had the power to deprive her of that feeling.

My client is a singer. I asked her if she was practicing her music, which I knew was something she loved. She was not. Was she taking walks in the park? Being in nature was another one of the activities that brought her joy and made her feel connected. She was not. Was she getting together with friends? Again, the answer was no. Was she going to her church? By now she knew what I was up to, and we both fell silent. My client had stopped nourishing herself with anything meaningful or delicious, all the while frantically scrolling forward and backward, looking for deliciousness online. My client had stopped paying attention to herself and instead turned herself over to the computer to deliver someone who would pay attention to her. She had stopped loving herself, when what she wanted was to feel loved. She saw the contradiction immediately. When presented with the invitation to reclaim her heart and resume an active role in taking care of herself, she was flooded with tears. Turning toward her own heart was itself an act of love.

What happened with my client is not unusual. Technology lures us into unconsciousness, and before we know it, we have surrendered to a virtual life, a potential virtual mate, a possible virtual community, a prospective virtual professional network. But the more we try to subsist on the fumes of the virtual, the more frantic we become for something of substance, something real.

Many people now relate to the Internet as if it were a kind of savior and have stopped looking to themselves to provide what they need and want. As we become more dependent upon technology, we also need to continue to employ our own intelligence and imaginations mindfully and not give up the effort that self-care requires. We have become actively passive under the guise of being virtually active, believing that we are taking care of ourselves when we are in fact abandoning responsibility for meeting our own needs and thus abandoning ourselves.

There is nothing wrong with looking for a mate or a new community of like-minded companions or colleagues on the Internet, nothing wrong with trying to get our needs met with the assistance of technology. Technology can be a tool in our self-care toolbox, but we still need to know how to take care of ourselves without technology. We need to ask ourselves questions such as:

- What am I experiencing in this moment?

- What nourishes me?

- What is the experience or feeling I am longing for?

- What might I offer myself to create that feeling
  or experience?

Such questions are a way to become more intimate with what we really need, a fundamental part of the self-care. In truth, we are our own best caretakers, better than any technology could ever be, but we have to reclaim that role, trust our capacity to fill it, and then make the genuine effort that real self-care requires.

Begin to reclaim that role for yourself by turning the power off and asking yourself, *What do I need?* Pause and listen to what comes. Sense your direct experience. Next, ask the same question, but this time specifically addressing your heart, placing your hand there as you ask, *What does my heart long for?* Notice if your heart's response is different from your mind's response. Now repeat the process and ask first, your mind, and then again, your heart, *How can I best take care of myself?* Let these questions marinate without demanding answers. The answers will make themselves known when they are ready.

19

the umbilical cord of technology

Jane doesn't love her partner. She hasn't loved him for a long time. She stays in the relationship primarily because he fixes her computer when it breaks. She can't or doesn't want to face the hassle, the difficulty, the horror of having to find a new repair person every time her Internet connection fails, her smartphone won't sync, her computer gets a virus, or any of the other many technology-based problems that now arise. Not wanting this, she imagines herself waiting for days without service, in the dark, isolated and cut off from the world until someone from the Geek Squad arrives. Adding to her dread is Jane's certainty that she'll be left with a broken computer, no partner, and no way of finding another intimate relationship because her broken computer will leave her without a link to the world. When Jane imagines her life without her partner—or, more accurately, without her partner there to fix her technology—she experiences fear and despair. Her relationship with her technology keeps her imprisoned in the belief that she is unable to take care of herself.

Michael is a seventy-five-year-old widower. He didn't grow up with technology or even use it in the latter part of his career, and he wouldn't have any desire to understand it now except that his family lives in another part of the country and he needs to feel part of his family's daily life. His family is his lifeline. He wants to see pictures of his grandchildren and be kept in the loop of what is going on with his adult children. But he must communicate with his family in the way that they now engage, which means emailing, texting, and using social media. In order for Michael to take advantage of the benefits technology provides, he has to be able to participate in the online world.

Digital media skills need to be in his seventy-five-year-old wheelhouse if he is to remain in the embrace of family. The onus is on him to figure it out.

Michael is, like many elderly people, more than a little afraid and a lot resistant to technology. Learning to operate electronics is not the way he wants to spend the twilight of his life, and yet what it can bring him is what he most values. So he's caught between a rock and a hard place. His fear and agitation about this are palpable when you're with him. He learns how to get access to the family Facebook page but then a moment later is unable to get there again. He opens a photo but then can't get out of the program. He doesn't retain the information, and because he lives alone, he has no one to help him figure things out each time he gets stuck. The situation can make him feel desperate, isolated, and helpless, at a time in his life when he already feels these things too often.

In a study by researchers at the University of Cambridge and British telco giant BT, it was discovered that one-third of people now feel "overwhelmed" by technology. A Virgin Digital Help survey found that six in ten people consider technology confusing and stressful.[1] It is not uncommon to hear intelligent people describe how disempowered they feel by their personal technology systems, which are increasingly extensive and complex. The task of simply making our technology work properly can be daunting in and of itself. Every day a new computer virus appears, a new digital dilemma, malware, incident of hacking or of cyberterrorism—you name it, it's out there, lurking somewhere in our cybermidsts, and it's just a matter of time until it hits our own systems. The host of technological issues that we must now be able to decipher and solve is astounding. We've come a long way since a fifteen-year-old created the first computer virus in 1982.[2]

Like Jane, we are becoming increasingly and unnervingly dependent upon those who manage our technology, not only because of the complexity it entails but also because it seems that every malfunction in our computer now has the potential to wipe out our lives. "My entire life is on that computer!" is a common reaction to a frozen computer. It is often through tears of despair that we wail,

"The wheel just won't stop spinning!" People describe their approach to the Genius Bar at the Apple Store as if they were approaching the pearly gates. When the twenty-something computer genius says, "I'll take a look at it," we struggle to keep ourselves upright and not drop to our knees in gratitude. We need our technology, and the possibility of becoming completely isolated when we lose our technological connection terrifies us.

The culture of a society determines which traits we most value and thus perpetuate. At one time in history, a woman chose her mate on the basis of his ability to hunt and bring meat home for the family. At another time, she chose a mate on the basis of his ability to hold a steady job, so that she could be sure she and her children would be taken care of. At a primal level, we choose our life partners on the basis of what will keep us safe and improve our chances of survival. More and more, what I hear these days in my office is that what makes a man good marriage material is his ability to navigate the drop-down menu, understand the cPanel, and, above all, get us back online. Functioning technology means survival. When we select our mates on the basis of this ability, we effectively breed this trait into the species, sending this DNA forward through our children. While future generations may be less empathic because they stare into screens and not the faces of real people, they will undoubtedly be skilled at making their computers work.

For those who are living in emotionally unsatisfying but technologically reassuring relationships, or who feel intimidated, helpless, and controlled by technology, it is important to reclaim a sense of empowerment. To feel calm, we need to feel we can understand how our lives function, and these days, that has to include our technology. While it is understandable to want to just throw the whole technology problem out the window, assume the fetal position, and turn it over to someone who will take it off our plates, this approach engenders a sense of fragility and fear. It is not only uncomfortable but also ungrounding and unnerving to feel we need something we also fear and don't understand. Throwing up our hands leads us to do things that we don't want to do, like stay in relationships that we don't want to be in and depend on people we don't want to depend on. We're naturally upset by the trade-off that such a dependency entails. It's also true that if we choose to remain ignorant about our technology, we are choosing to relinquish other important choices as well, choices we might not relinquish if we were to consider them consciously.

Learning about our own technology, oddly, is now a form of self-care. Just a little bit of understanding goes a long way in making us feel like we can take care of ourselves. This knowledge grounds us so that we don't feel like we are flailing about in cyberspace, relying on something we don't understand, can't touch, and can't see. We don't have to be able to understand or manage all of it, but we can dip our toes into the digital waters and build a slightly more friendly and less fearful relationship with technology. Over time, we can also build a network of people and services to help us navigate the cyberworld, so that when our systems do fail, we have a plan for how to proceed. At the end of the day, being able to take care of ourselves in ways that are fundamental to our well-being—which now includes technology—earns us back our freedom.

my smartphone and me

This past weekend, my daughter, a tween, received a text from a friend asking for the address of a girl they both know. At the time of the text all three were in the same room on a playdate; the girl whose address the friend wanted was actually sitting three feet away from the friend. My daughter responded with a very wise question: "Why don't you look up from your screen and ask her yourself?"

On playdates nowadays, children are choosing to play with their devices instead of one another. On a recent date of eleven-year-olds, I watched as all three girls got on their individual devices within a minute of convening. Their social interaction, at least the interactive portion of it, came to a halt. When I pointed out to one of the fathers what I was witnessing, it was clear from his expression and smile that he didn't find it to be troublesome or strange—three friends, all staring at their private screens, not talking to or looking at one another. In fact, he later commented on how cute the girls are and how much they share as friends. It seems the meaning of the word *share* has also changed with the advent of the digital age. *Share* no longer means what it used to in relation to friendship—the internal meeting ground that is built by people relating with one another, creating the emotional connections. Now it seems *sharing* refers to having similar preferences for and within technology, as in liking similar apps, models, cases, servers, and so on, as well as sharing the space from which you use technology individually—together.

I recently asked a woman in her twenties what the term *party* means for her generation, as well as what she and her friends talk about and do when they get together. I learned that at group gatherings for twenty-somethings and also teenagers, many are busy "socializing" on their devices—that is, texting people who are not actually present at the party. There is a lot of attention paid to the devices in the room and who else is where else and doing what else. The people *in* the room seem to be of less interest than who or what might be happening elsewhere. This report is consistent with what others of her generation say. It seems that a "party" is now a shared physical space in which to play alone on individual devices, communicating with people in other physical spaces. This is not to be confused with a "Twitter party," which does not even require a shared physical space for its party status.

I don't attend a lot of parties these days, but I did used to go to what felt a little bit like a party when I took my children to music school. There was a great old farm table in the front room where we parents waited during our children's lessons. For years, it was where conversations and laughter mixed with the sounds of pianos and violins wafting down from the upper floors. It wasn't a place to wait so much as a place to be together. But lately, at that same table, each week you'll find ten humans and ten devices: twenty of us being "together." The only sounds emerging from the room come from keypads being tapped, a phone vibrating against the wood of the table, and the occasional ringtone or blip from a device someone forgot to silence. The sounds of technology have replaced the sounds of conversation and connection. The party is over.

In truth, every form of social interaction is being altered by technology. A digital device is now a permanent presence in our interactions. A woman friend, almost forty, is single and interested in meeting a man. She tried online dating for some time but in the end felt agitated and disillusioned. She sensed she was wasting time on nothing. If she had to be single, she would rather be single and get to do what she wanted to do with her time, as opposed to being single and also having to waste her time on terrible dates. And yet the problem, as she saw it, was that she still wanted to meet someone and was saddened and worried by the idea of quitting altogether. I knew that she was a gastronome and also liked to eat out, so I suggested that maybe once a week she could have dinner alone at a restaurant in her neighborhood. She could eat at the bar, try some new dishes, and see what transpired. It wouldn't be too much trouble, since it was something she already enjoyed.

After a couple of months I checked in to see how it was going. She told me that the experiment had been a failure. She had not met any new men despite dining at the bar alone once a week, as I'd suggested. Though not necessary for this story, it is worth noting that my friend, in addition to being single, is also smart, funny, stylish, warm, and very pretty, so it was hard to understand why no one would approach her. I asked her to talk me through, in some detail, her nights at the restaurant. She said that she'd arrive at a local restaurant-bar at around 9:00 p.m., order a glass of wine and some dinner, and usually leave by about 10:30 p.m. That was it. And then she happened to slip in one more very important detail.

As it turns out, her solo dinners were not solo at all. She was having dinner with her iPhone, gazing into it throughout the entire meal. So as not to feel embarrassed for being alone or look like a person who (heaven forbid) was there to try to meet someone, she had found a way to remove all vulnerability (and possibility) by appearing to be a "winner" with her eyes glued to her device. Ticking away on it, she looked like someone with a full life, with an uninterrupted stream of friends and engaging materials coming in. With that busy a device, one could only guess that she was eating at the bar because her life was so full she had no time to shop for groceries. Like a lover locked in an intimate exchange, my friend was staring deep into the "i" of her iPhone, all the while imagining and wishing that a human would enter her space. But between her plate and her device, where was the space for another to enter?

I made a second suggestion then: that, going forward, she bring a book (paper, not Kindle) to the restaurant. And while she was at it, that she leave her device in her bag, out of sight. Amazingly, since trading in her iPhone for a book, the number of humans (specifically men) who have approached her has risen exponentially. This experiment supports the experience that so many people describe. Technology, with its countless opportunities for communication, also closes the door to communication with those around us. It seals us in behind it.

The relationship we have with our devices is monogamous. The way we use our technology is not socially porous and does not leave space for others to enter. We relate to our devices as if they were new lovers: we can't take our eyes off of them, can't stand to be away from them, and want to be "on" them all day and night. One woman told me that when she forgets her phone, she feels as if a part of her is missing. Our devices complete us. Whatever we focus our attention and energy on will grow, right? We nourish that to which we bring our attentive gaze. At this time in history, our gaze is nourishing the technology in our lives—and at the same time, our dependency upon it, both practical and emotional. As we spend more time relating with our devices, we spend less time relating with the people in our lives. Our devices are leading us into social isolation, though we're in constant communication and unceasingly "connected."

How do we want to live? Are we comfortable becoming a society in which most of the time most of our members are looking down at their screens, lost in their private universes, their attention elsewhere? Are we going to check the "yes" box to becoming a community whose members have gone MIA, their bodies remaining but the people in them having left the scene? Furthermore, do we want to give up our collective and connected societal space and the shared experience of life that includes the other people in our physical world? We must ask ourselves what we really need from our fellow travelers on Earth and whether being in connection with those around us is still integral to our sense of well-being.

If the answer is that we are not okay becoming a society of presence-snatched shells, then we need to become mindful first and foremost of our own behavior. If we still want, and maybe even need, a world in which we experience life together, then we ourselves, individually, need to look away from our screens and enter the physical world we are in. If we want the world outside us to wake up, then we need to wake up to the world inside and outside ourselves. If we want the people around us to be available and present, then we need to show up and be available and present. It all begins and ends with the choices we make for ourselves.

Right now, make the choice to bring your attention to the sounds that you are hearing in this moment. Whatever sounds come up, just let your ears receive, effortlessly, whatever arises. Don't try to choose among the sounds or figure out what's causing them. Notice instead how the hearing just happens, without your having to do anything at all. Spend one full minute listening, experiencing sound, and being right here.

Make it a practice to notice and experience each of the five senses, intimately and individually, every day. Start a ritual of stopping and dropping in. Throughout the day, deliberately stop what you are doing and drop your attention into your body. Spend at least one minute smelling what you smell, one minute tasting what you taste, one minute feeling what you feel in your body, one minute seeing what you see, noticing your environment, and one minute hearing what you hear—five different practices that require only five minutes total of time.

The benefit of this very simple and short practice is that it shepherds you instantly into the present moment, which is the only place or time that you can be in relationship with others or yourself. Nothing and no one can enter your life if you are not here to experience it.

21

reawakening to the
world we share

Years ago, Ralph Waldo Emerson wrote about the potential negative effects of relying on clocks as a replacement for noticing
where the sun is on the horizon.[1] Today, many of the young
people I ask have no idea that the time of day is even related to where
the sun is sitting in the sky. Time is simply a number that appears on
a smartphone, connected to nothing else. The fact that we can't figure
out the time of day by the placement of the sun is not a disaster, but
have we stopped noticing the sun at all and thereby lost the awareness
that a connection between the sun and time even exists? The more we
ignore our physical environment, the more we lose touch with the
relationship that exists among the elements of life, of which we are
one. It is not just time that is being removed from its connection with
nature and the universe as a whole: we seem to have taken ourselves
out of relationship with all that we are in fact interconnected with and
rely upon.

When you glance around the streets and public transportation
these days, most people are staring into their small screens. Few are
noticing the sky, the buildings, faces, flowers, or anything else. We're
no longer aware of where we are in relationship with our physical
world. Our world has been narrowed down to our devices, no longer
inclusive of our larger environment.

At a very basic level, noticing our environment keeps us safe. Looking up from our screens when we cross the street protects us from
oncoming traffic. On a subtler level, when we notice what is around
us, when we are present and aware of the larger world we are living in,

we are saying yes to life, to participating fully in it and not just in our small world as it appears on our small screens. When our attention widens, our world widens with it, and when our attention is perpetually narrowed onto a small screen, our world shrinks to meet it. So, too, when we are present to what is happening around us, new experiences can occur. We can meet new people, see something that we have never seen, discover and taste a fresh experience, grow and change. When we open to the world around us, the world opens to us. Being available and awake to our environment turns the present moment into an adventure, adding spontaneity and unknowableness to life, little of which is possible when we are consumed with our devices, scrolling and selecting from one screen menu to the next. Being open to the larger environment allows the world to enter us and us to enter it. In fact, while we are busy searching for something lively on our smartphones, we are missing out on the real liveliness that is all around us.

We so often feel disconnected and separate these days precisely because we are disconnected and separate from where we physically are and everything that that includes. We don't feel part of our environment because we are not behaving as if we are a part of our environment. We are connecting only to our devices and then wondering why we feel connected only to our devices. But our devices are not a source of true human connectedness, and they don't engender a larger sense of well-being. We cannot feel part of the world through just our screens. Indeed, in order to feel truly well, we need to feel connected to something more than just technology.

Being present where we are in our physical world allows us to remember our inherent interdependence and where we fit into this group dance that is life. When we join the physical world, we notice the other people with whom we share our space and our planet and with whom we might share a smile, a conversation, or a frustration. We notice the less fortunate lying in doorways, remember what we have that they don't, and maybe consider how we can make things better. We see buildings that other people's fathers and mothers built. We become aware of foods that people from other countries harvested. We observe the trees, which make it possible for us to breathe. We take in the sky and remember that we are just little dots spinning on one planet in one solar system in one universe among so many others. We see ourselves in relation to and as a part of all of these other life-forms. When we look up from our screens, we realize ourselves as part of the world, not separate from it, precisely the feeling, ironically, that we are so often trying to get through technology.

Without this sense of interdependence, we are at risk of forgetting that we need one another and our planet, not only to feel connection and belonging but also, at a very basic level, to survive. Without this sense of interdependence, we can start believing that we need only our smartphones and at least one good digit with which to tap the icons. But this is not the case. To feel grounded and well, we need each other. Our interconnectedness is at the center of our humanness. Quite simply, we need to put our devices down and look up from our screens, wake up to where we are, reclaim our presence in the physically grounded world, and reconnect with the environment that we are in and the people we are in it with. To feel that we are really in life, part of life, we need to start showing up for life with our presence, recognizing and participating in the interconnected and interdependent matrix that is our physically shared world. Take a moment now to contemplate all the different people and efforts, all that had to happen, for you to be in the space that you are in at this moment.

22

all alone in virtual community

recently asked a young woman why she spent so much time playing The Sims 3, a virtual-character video game. She told me she likes the sense of community it offers her. She feels less cooped up in her own home and more a part of the world when she plays. She goes out into the neighborhood and walks around, sees other people in their houses, and gets a sense of the community. The neighborhood she is talking about is a virtual one, of course. When I reminded her that the people she was looking at in those homes are not real and that the neighborhood she wanders around in is also fake, she laughed and said she knew all that, but it didn't bother her.

When I first heard composer Eric Whitacre talk about the debut of his virtual choir on YouTube, I got the chills.[1] This virtual choir is a collection of individual voices recorded in different physical locations and then woven together online to create one choir, as if the singers had actually sung together. First, I was chilled by the music of "Lux Aurumque" ("Light and Gold"), which is heartbreaking and captivating. Like all great music, it has the power to connect us with our own divinity. But then this virtual choir also injected me with a dose of isolation and a fear of what this kind of composition could mean for the human experience. My blood ran cold.

Whitacre has assembled a technological collage of sound and sight that is remarkable, but other than the project involving music and humans, it has little to do with the experience that takes place in an actual real-life choir. There is a magical and transcendent experience that happens when we come together as human beings to create music, side by side, heart to heart, an experience that Whitacre himself describes as life changing—it was the first time he felt a part of something larger. The magic and mystery of the experience are a result of living something together, cocreating and sharing an experience as it unfolds before us, larger than and containing us. When we come together as individuals in a creative process, we become a part of the larger whole, our separateness melting into the experience itself, into one another. We become vehicles for the universe to express itself through our seemingly separate embodiments.

When we omit the *together* part of the experience, when the process no longer happens *together*, it's no longer shared—we cut out the key ingredient in the experience, entirely change its nature, and extract its very soul. As I witnessed Whitacre conducting alone in front of a black screen in silence, as I watched the singers' faces float by in individual boxes—a mosaic of separate lives pieced together in the ether, creating the illusion of connectedness—I knew that I would rather *feel* the connection directly than be left with the *thought* that I had lived it. And I wondered: is this what the future holds? It felt apocalyptic.

The virtual choir informs its participants that they have become part of something larger than themselves, that they were indeed connected. But in the experience of creating it, they were actually alone and disconnected. The experience of the virtual choir, to use Whitacre's own words, is an expression of "souls on their own desert islands sending electronic messages in bottles to each other."[2] I believe he used this image to suggest a kind of optimism about humanity and our longing to connect. But I didn't find his analogy to be optimistic, nor do I see sending out electronic messages from my own desert island as an acceptable substitute for experiencing real connection. To celebrate the virtual choir is to celebrate the end of the direct experience of connection. It is to say that, going forward, we agree to be nourished by the *concept* of connection and to let technology "live fully" instead, while we humans stand by and hear about it, delighting in our ability to recreate something that looks like real connection but isn't.

In one particularly disturbing testimonial, a singer wrote about how wonderful the virtual choir was because she got to sing with her sister.[3] It can be wonderful to be able to listen to your sister's voice in unity with your own, and yet there is a cultural amnesia setting in, a forgetting of what direct experience is. In truth, this young woman did not sing *with* her sister. They did not have the experience of singing together: each sister sang alone. What this singer lived was something entirely different. She had the experience of knowing that recordings of her and her sister's voices were brought together in a technological feat. It looks and sounds like she and her sister were singing together, and it's that simulation of reality, that notion of being together, that she gets to take home as an experience.

"People will go to any lengths necessary to find and connect with each other. It doesn't matter the technology," says Whitacre.[4] Yes, people are desperate for connection, but it *does* matter the technology. Technology is replacing the direct experience of connection with the idea and simulation of connection, and what worries me is that we humans seem to be losing our capacity to appreciate the difference. After listening to the virtual choir, I am left with a haunting echo—the sound of humans singing alone into empty rooms, like lost birds calling out for their mothers to find them and bring them home. And I can't help but wonder if the haunting comes not only from the poignancy of the music but also from the poignancy of what's at risk of being lost.

The problem is not that we are creating new sources of community but that virtual communities often cannot offer the same emotional nourishment that physical or real communities can. It's vital that we remain aware of this important difference. There is nothing wrong with a virtual choir, but we need to remember the inimitable value of singing and being together in real life!

When the waitress at the local diner asks us if we want our "usual" or the coffee cart barista notices that we weren't there the morning before, such experiences make us feel grounded and connected—and happy. People describe a great sense of contentment and security when they experience themselves as being known in their shared physical world. On the other hand, many clients and friends report feeling empty, unsatisfied, and lonely after hours of participating in virtual communities, precisely the opposite of the experience they crave and that physical communities provide. Sadly, with technology we risk winning the world but losing our village. We can be part of a community made up of people all over the world but not talk to the few people who share a bus stop with us every morning. Though *known about* by everyone, we are increasingly *known by* no one. According to research conducted at the Center for Cognitive & Social Neuroscience at the University of Chicago, the more face-to-face interactions we have, the less lonely we are, while the more online interactions we have (the sort that don't lead to face-to-face contact), the more lonely we are.[5]

Virtual communities have benefits, but they also have the capacity to change the way we relate to our real-life experiences. Many of us are now less committed to and dependent upon this moment of being together for our sense of connection and emotional nourishment. Physical interaction has even become an impediment to our engaging with technology. We have to hurry up and finish with the people in front of us so that we can get back to tweeting and texting to people elsewhere. The system has flipped: people are now the distraction, and our online world is the main stage.

At one time, the makers of technology may have intended for it to bring people together, to create actual connection and a richer experience of life. Regardless of the original intention, however, it seems that the system has turned on itself. Recent studies have found that despite being more connected than ever, people feel more alone than ever. As Sherry Turkle, a social psychologist at the Massachusetts Institute of Technology, puts it, "People are more connected to each other than ever before in human history. . . . But they're also more lonely and distant from one another in their unplugged lives. We are doing more connecting, but feeling more disconnected."[6] Surprisingly, those who report feeling most alone are young people under thirty-five, the most prolific social networkers of all.[7] We sit alone at our screens, our desert islands, while the invisible wires and cables get to do the interacting. We believe that our computers' connections are our own. But the more we congratulate ourselves on our ability to simulate the experience of being human, the more the direct experience of being human slips away, little by little.

It is not an either-or situation. Even with online communities as part of our life, we still need to come together physically to feel and be in one another's presence. We can participate in online communities, but we can't substitute the online experience for the in-person experience. Being in the same room and sharing space with other people stays with us and becomes part of our cellular makeup in a way that is different from sharing something at a distance through the computer. We need to remember that virtual communities do not feed us on a bodily and heartfelt level in the same way that real communities do.[8] Bodies respond to other bodies. The heart responds to direct human contact.

The young woman who is deriving her sense of community by wandering through a virtual neighborhood, walking her virtual dog, and looking into the houses of virtual characters is not building the connective tissue that real community offers. I am not suggesting that we throw away our virtual communities; they serve a purpose. But, rather, we need to honor the value, nourishment, and joy that come from spending time in one another's company, actually sharing something together. And in order to achieve that, we need to consciously make time to be together with others in one physical place as the embodied creatures that we are. Even with all the virtual connecting that's happening, we still need the richness that can come only from sharing physical space. Physical and emotional presence are the building blocks of community. Both require effort, but it is effort wisely invested and unmistakably rewarded.

PART
3

our relationship
with ourselves

23

is your smartphone stealing your life?

These days, at children's events, the large majority of parents are participating in the experience from behind a digital device. Recently, I looked around my child's dance studio to find almost every adult jockeying for a good sightline for their smartphone or other device, as they tried to capture images of their children dancing while they, the doting parents, simultaneously missed seeing the actual dance. Preoccupied, futzing with their focus controls, adjusting buttons, and swiping screens, these event-recording parents never really see their offspring living their salient moments—accepting their diplomas, playing their sonatas, scoring goals. In essence, these parents are "tech-ing" their way through their children's lives.

I wager we probably miss half of our experiences while trying to figure out how to preserve them. This is because we want to possess our experiences the way we would an object. And, indeed, we end up possessing just that: a recording of an experience that wasn't directly experienced. We have something we can hold onto and show—yes, it is ours to some degree—but we don't have the true felt sense of those experiences in our lives.

A therapy clients pulls out her smartphone whenever we start getting into emotional material. She does this, she says, so that she can remember what we are talking about, to have it for later. She wants a record of her experience, a report on her feelings, and she gets this in exchange for actually getting to feel her feelings and experience her experience. In this way, technology serves as a perfect partner to the mind, as they have the same goals. With her experience avoided in real life, but logged neatly in her notes folder, my client can stay exactly who she has always been, firmly identified with her mind and with the added pleasure of having something else to think about. Her life is stored behind an icon—unlived. With the help of her device, she has found a way to successfully avoid not only her own experience but also my empathy and a deepened relationship with me as her therapist—which, if she were able to feel it, might actually allow her to change.

A report that I now frequently hear in my psychotherapy practice is that people feel estranged from life, not present as it is happening, and not the one who lived it once it has happened. As one woman expressed it, it's like being "a ghost, floating outside of life," aware of it but not in it. While we know intellectually that our lives are happening and time is passing, we are not exactly sure that we are the ones who are living it, at least not directly. *Internal absence is the disease of the digital age.* It's as if the rise in technology's presence has caused our own presence in life to go missing.

Bodily felt memories arise organically from simply being in our lives as they are happening. When we record life through technology, however, we end up with a lot of technology—16 GB of memory—but no bodily felt memories that become part of us at a cellular level. Our phones are full, but we feel empty.

There is nothing unhealthy about wanting to take pictures of our lives, to keep memories in a tangible form. But with the ubiquity of tech devices, many of us are now taking the pictures in lieu of being present and attentive to the experiences we are recording. Taking the photographs has become the primary experience, not a momentary diversion away from it. Experiences lived through a recording device are not integrated into our being, the way they are when we watch them with only our own eyes. When we are removed from our experiences, our experiences are removed from us, and we cannot feel them directly. How can we feel like we are in our lives if we are not in them when they are occurring—when we're behind our devices instead, with our attention focused on our screens? Such a life feels unreal, and as a result, we need our devices to play life back to us to make it seem real.

To state the obvious: in order to feel present in our lives, we have to be present in our lives. When we refuse the sweetness and nourishment that is life directly experienced, it's no wonder we are starved for the feeling of being alive. We miss out on this great adventure that our smartphones proudly display. Our lives exist in our iPhoto files, but not inside ourselves.

The desire to capture life is motivated primarily by fear. We are afraid that if we stop trying to capture life, to pin it down and prepare it to be remembered—often before it has even happened—we will miss out on it or it will go away. We are afraid of the impermanence that is the very nature of life, the fact that every moment is born and then dies into the next, that nothing, not even our most memorable experiences, can be lived forever. In truth, we are always living with birth and death. Our minds, however, desperately want to create ground and permanence, to discover something that doesn't come and go, something we can keep. The recording device is the mind's tool for trying to create this permanence. The device gives us the false sense that we can solidify our moments and keep them from disappearing into the constantly flowing river that life is. How ironic that in an effort to hold onto our experience, prevent it from slipping through our fingers, we perform the ultimate sacrifice and disappear ourselves from the experience, stop living it directly.

In order to feel *in* our lives, to experience life fully, we must be willing to let the moment go and welcome it again when it appears in a new guise. The challenge is that we are not trained in this way of living, not okay with letting anything go. We want to keep things, deny the passage of time and the ephemeral nature of all experience. We use our devices to try to freeze life and make it stay. But only our own presence can stay constant. All experience that passes through our presence, no matter how many copies we make out of it, will change and disappear. Let me repeat that: Only our own presence can stay constant. All experience that passes through it, no matter how many copies we make out of it, will change and disappear. Chances are that even though I said that twice and you may even have had an "Aha!" moment, you will forget it in another couple of pages. Such is the nature of experience.

What if, instead of dispatching our smartphones to hold onto our children's recitals (and our children in the process), we simply showed up, completely present with our loving attention rather than our devices? What if instead of trying not to lose our experiences, we took the chance to lose ourselves, to disappear into our experiences? How meaningful would life become if, rather than trying to stock-pile pieces of it and deny its transience, we could allow ourselves to be fully available and *in* it when it is here, and then let it go, having lived it completely?

Try this exercise: Pick an event that you would normally experience through a recording device, and then later through the recorded video, and see what it's like to go without recording that experience—to show up technologically naked, if you will. Simply be there at the event, fully present, fully attentive. Experience it directly, without technology separating you from it. Notice if the lived experience of the event is different when you watch it through your own eyes, without the distraction of the device. Notice, too, how you hold and integrate the experience going forward and if that too feels different from how you hold a recorded experience.

If the experiment proves irrelevant, nothing is lost, except maybe one recital not making it to your video file. It's easy enough to pick your smartphone back up and begin recording your life again, saving it for later. But be open to the possibility that you may not want to get out of the pool—not after you have felt what it's like to go for a swim in your own life, without a suit! See what it's like simply to live life as it is unfolding, without trying to grasp it or hold it in any one shape, without reminding yourself later what the "experience" was like. Watch as life continually changes and transforms itself, and see how you can roll right along with it, just showing up for the shape that life is in right now and that you are in right now. The idea that we could hold the moment in any one shape or that we will lose out on it if we don't pin it down is an illusion. The only thing that we can control is whether we show up wholeheartedly in the moment as it unfolding.

24

i tweet, therefore i am

employ a lot of young people: babysitters, nannies, homework helpers, tutors, birthday party performers, athletic trainers, music teachers, and many others. I am continually surrounded by young people, to say nothing of my own children, their friends, and the children of my adult friends. In my therapy practice, too, I work with many people in their twenties and thirties. With this great pool of resources available to me, I am constantly witnessing, dialoguing, and inquiring about the experiences young people are living in today's virtual world.

An experience that I frequently hear young people describe is that of not being real or being alienated from their own life—as if they themselves are somehow virtual. Because their work and social lives happen virtually and so much of their self-identity is crafted online, many feel as if their lives are a simulation of real lives, as if they are unreal characters in an online game. The question I am often asked is "When is my real life going to happen?" In a particularly extreme example (which I will never forget), one young woman felt so unreal to herself that she was compelled to get her arms and legs X-rayed to prove to herself that she (or something solid) actually existed behind her image.

It is a regular event now for me, as a therapist, to be presented with a smartphone during a session, which my client (often while kneeling at my feet) will scroll through in order to display to me their most important experiences. While clients have periodically brought in photos throughout the years, these shared selfies, which now play an active role in many therapy discussions, seem to accomplish a different purpose. Such digital representations of my clients' lives serve as both a kind of substitute for and a legitimization of their experiences.

The images provide them with a sense of being someone who is indeed living a real life, and the fact that I can see it too, right there on their smartphone, makes it real for them and for me as well.

An interesting thing happens for these young people in the process of witnessing their lives in digital images: they become even more disconnected from their own experiences and often more alienated from their true feelings. They've become the object of their own experiences rather than the subject. With technology now a part of every experience we undergo, we have become a society of people watching ourselves, and so we need proof of our own existence to know that we are not virtual—like our world. Nothing feels real unless it has been captured in an image and subsequently played back for us.

It appears that technology is returning us to that stage of infancy when we ceased to exist in our own inner world if we were not mirrored back through our mother's eyes. With technology leading the way, we are creating an adult infancy, a state of being where no self-experience exists until and unless it is reflected back to us. We believe ourselves *to be* when we see ourselves *having been*. The experience of our lives is increasingly being created by a lens and felt only through its reflection. The digital device is our new mother, creating our existence and showing us how, and indeed that, we feel.

Before technology became central to our lives, we often experienced our lives privately. We might have done something kind for a stranger on the street, for which the other person was grateful. It could have been a simple, sweet moment, perhaps even a profound one, shared between two people who would never meet again. And that was it—the whole event. We lived it, absorbed it, integrated it, all within ourselves only and all without texting a soul about it. We had many moments that we never shared with anyone, never reported or posted anywhere, which then became part of us. These moments were fundamentally integrated into who we were, and through their integration we changed and evolved.

These days, the instant something happens, we are immediately on our devices, texting everyone we know to tell the story of who we are, the story of our lives. After the personal texts have gone out, we start posting on social media. As soon as we are finished getting it out to the world, we start checking to see the responses coming in about it. In a sense, the whole event, our life, takes place outside of us and on the screen; life is not something we live directly but rather something we use to establish our self-image and existence.

Other than when we're taking off on an airplane, there are very few moments these days when we are left to process experiences for ourselves, without the immediate feedback that comes through technology. And yet it is often in the alone time that our experiences are able to sink in and we absorb them, take ownership and make them our own, make them real. When we immediately text to announce everything that happens to us, we are effectively giving away our experiences, disallowing them from becoming part of us, rejecting the opportunity to really taste them. We demand validation for our experiences before we have even ingested them, mistakenly believing that the nourishment will come through this kind of validation and not digestion. Our experiences are immediately turned into sound bites that say something *about* us, but in the process we relinquish the opportunity to make such experiences *part* of us.

If we live something and it is only known or witnessed privately—not texted, posted, or tweeted to anyone else—is it real? Did it happen? In a virtual world, where so much of what we interact with is not physical or tangible, where we can put on Google Glass or HoloLens and feel like we are experiencing something that our body is not actually living, what it means to be "real" is no longer clear.

What will be the result of all this augmented reflection? How will we evolve and change as a species if we become reliant on our devices to experience our lives and to know that we are real? Perhaps at some point we will evolve into devices ourselves, become technology, the human being existing only in digital form. Perhaps we will end up merging the real and the reflection of the real. And yet, for now, while we are still trying to navigate the gap between the two, still trying to make ourselves and our experiences feel real, we need to address the issue head on. We need to find ways, other than X-raying ourselves, to trust that we are indeed here.

The next time something happens in your life, notice what it feels like to hold it alone for a little while—that is, to not tell anyone about it and keep it just for yourself. Focus on simply experiencing it, sensing any feelings, thoughts, or body sensations that the event creates. As you do this, try to refrain from preparing the story of what happened in your mind, packaging the tale that you will soon send out to the world.

The exercise is simply to give yourself a little time just to live the experience for yourself, marinate in it, and let it take up residence in your own body. By practicing this basic exercise regularly, we can relearn how to directly experience our own lives, to absorb their contents for and by ourselves, and, in the process, feel the realness of our own presence in the world—without a single person in the audience.

25

branding the self

S omeone recently asked me if I plan on using my book to sell my brand—and as long as we were discussing it, they wanted to know what *is* my brand. I was unnerved by the question and left wondering how the act of writing a book—that is, writing what interests me—is different from writing what would "demonstrate" what interests me or, for that matter, who I am. "The purpose of your life is to sell your brand," this same person explained, which she managed to do, I might add, without cracking a smile. Of course, people in the business of promoting need to know how they are going to sell your product and you with it, but these days, the selling of the self is not just about generating sales—it has become a national epidemic.

What does it mean to brand ourselves, anyway? Kleenex means tissue; the brand *is* the product. Martha Stewart is a certain look, smell, and experience. To brand ourselves is to turn ourselves into a product—something that is a knowable and repeatable experience, something that can be described in a thirty-second elevator pitch.

Before social media, before we felt pressured to become a brand, we didn't need to constantly tell the world, "This is what I am about; this is what I stand for." To be seen and known as who we are used to be an obvious by-product of simply *being* who we are. We *were* it, as opposed to having to *show* we were it. There was a seamless quality to the experience of living. Now, rather than just living life from the inside out, we stand outside our lives, pointing at ourselves and offering up a press kit on who we are.

With technology providing a constant screen on which to project our "me" image, we now relate to ourselves in the third person, as a product, and one that, in an ideal world, will go viral. Indeed, many of us have grown afraid that if we don't continually tell the world who we are, as everyone else is doing, we will become invisible and irrelevant. And if we stop the ongoing narrative about ourselves, stop being vigilant about our brand, we run the risk that who we are perceived as may not line up with how we want to be perceived. If this happens, our very sense of self is called into question.

I was recently on a spiritual retreat. The focus of the retreat was to let go of the ego self and to stop defending an idea of who we are—essentially, to become nobody. A couple of days into the silent retreat, we were alerted that a number of the participants had been on Facebook, breaking their internal silence by posting the fact that they were on silent retreat becoming spiritual people. I guess you could say their new brand was the brand of being nobody (maybe without a logo, too?). These folks were using social media as it is so often used: to establish an identity, announce who they are and what they stand for. They were busy becoming the best nobodies India had ever seen. They were on retreat to disappear as ego selves, but all the while they were using technology to make sure their disappeared selves were clearly visible to others.

I am in the habit of asking teenagers and young adults what they want to be when they grow up. It's been one of my favorite questions for more than a decade. In recent years, I have noticed that the answers I am receiving are changing, radically. It used to be that people almost always named a profession: "I want to be a basketball player . . . a singer in a band . . . a doctor . . . a teacher" and so forth. But now a new response is common: "I want to be famous." And when I ask, "Famous for what?" many of these young people look at me cockeyed, as if what they want to be famous for is something they've never considered. They respond as if the two questions don't belong together.

The Children's Digital Media Center recently determined that there was a strong link between children using social media and their valuing fame.[1] To be famous is not only a part of being a brand but also a brand unto itself—and the best kind, at that. To be recognized and known publicly is our purpose, and the experience of being seen is more important than the experience for which we are being seen. Our brands have replaced who we are.

The next time you are inclined to announce something about yourself on social media or a similar forum, try the following exercise. Pause before posting and use the impulse as an opportunity to practice mindfulness and become more self-aware. Ask yourself:

- Who is the person I am trying (want) to be seen as?

- Why is it important I be seen as that kind of person?

- Am I that kind of person?

- Is the "brand me" the same as the me who is creating the brand? If not, how are they different?

- What does my brand protect me from?

Next, write down several ways in which you define or present yourself—for example, "I am a lawyer . . . a mother . . . a soccer fan . . . a Democrat . . . a kind person," and the like. Now drop each statement that is a role you play, a description of you, or a thought, a belief, a feeling about yourself. Ask yourself:

- What if I didn't have to be that "somebody" all the time and didn't have to make people know I am that "somebody"?

- How am I different now, without those identities?

Notice what feelings arise. Do you feel free? Lost? Relieved? Empty?

And finally, as you go deeper into your inquiry, dip into the question that sits underneath all other questions: *Who am I?*

26

can you see me now?

A Facebook post by an intelligent friend, a fifty-year-old woman, read: "Up for an early bike ride, now followed up by some fresh fruit and an acai juice." Why do we now use our time to report such things? Why is it important that the public know our morning juice ritual? Do we not reap the same health benefits and take the same pride in that bike ride if others don't know about it? What has happened to the power of internal experience, the private knowing of what we do in our lives? It appears that internal validation is disappearing and we increasingly need an external response for each moment we live.

For every playdate my daughter attends, I receive handfuls of photos from both the caregivers and the parents, who diligently record the children's every slurp, skip, and hug. I am always delighted by pictures of my daughter, but there's a part of me that wishes children would be allowed to just get on with the business of playing and stop having to pause every few moments to play at playing so that the iPhone can get a playful shot, proving to everyone that playtime in fact happened.

At the pool this morning, a young man was playing ball with his father. After a few tosses, the boy started calling out to his friend, "We should get this on camera. It will be really cool to post," he said. But when his friend, who was busy on his own device, didn't capture the experience digitally, the ball toss with his dad simply faded out, as neither seemed interested in playing without the game being recorded—at least not once the idea of recording it was introduced. Without the ability to post it, the game was no longer worth playing; the value and fun of it had been drained away.

The rise of technology in our lives has been accompanied not only by the drive to turn ourselves into a brand but also by an undeniable explosion in our need to be witnessed. Everything we do, think, feel, eat, drink, and excrete has to be noticed and, with any virtual luck, "liked" by others, whether intimates or strangers. As one woman put it, without a witness and feedback, "what's the point really in doing it?" We give away our sense of validity when we offer up every aspect of our life to technology, and then, ironically, we depend upon that same technology to get our validity back. The way we're using technology has developed into both the cause of and solution to our invisibility.

Healthy childhood development involves a "look at me" stage during which children need everything they do to be witnessed and celebrated. "Watch me" is probably the phrase one hears the most often on any playground. This stage helps the child feel their own existence through the mirror of the parent's gaze and also helps them experience and demonstrate their developing strengths. At some point in healthy development, however, we begin to acknowledge our own experiences from the inside, to feel that we matter without needing to have everything reflected, and to maintain a sense of our existence without the mirror. While we still carry a healthy drive for acknowledgment in our adult lives—having our strengths and accomplishments noticed makes us feel seen, known, valued, and as though we belong—we outgrow having to shout, "Look at me!" every time we take a step or tie our shoes.

There is nothing wrong with wanting to have one's life witnessed and appreciated, particularly the things we feel proud of. And yet our healthy longing to be seen is metastasizing; our need for validation and visibility is becoming uncontrollable. And often what accompanies this swelling desire is the belief that everything we live, from every thought to every splinter, is of monumental significance and fascination to others. Paradoxically, the more we distrust the value and legitimacy of our own experience when it isn't witnessed, the more we seem to behave as if everything we do and think is of supreme importance.

Technology is giving us the means to indulge our infantile self-involvement, and it's causing us to lose the ability to discern what warrants an external witness and what needs to be experienced only by ourselves. There is a growing need for a witness to turn our lives into something that's worth living. Our devices, always available to be that witness, are now our meaning provider. We can have our device's undivided attention and adoring gaze whenever we want (save for a dead battery), and its attention alone, without any need for human contact, may at some point be all that is needed.

As both a psychotherapist and a human being living in this brave new digital world, I wonder about the roots of such changes. Are the children growing up in the digital age being denied proper parental acknowledgment? Are parents these days too focused on their private screens, too distracted talking into their Bluetooths, to be able to hear (or be bothered) when their children call out, "Watch me"? Or are the channels through which we are now trying to gain recognition insufficient to make us feel valuable? Maybe the one hundred birthday wishes we receive from Facebook friends (who have been reminded of our birthday by an alert on their computers) don't add up to the feeling that we matter.

Has technology fundamentally changed us so that we're now desperate for moment-to-moment validation to make ourselves and our lives matter? Are we now truly convinced that our switching from soy to skim lattés carries profound meaning? Or, on the other hand, is it that our basic nature has always been to want everything to be about ourselves, to be relentlessly acknowledged and celebrated, and that social media and technology have simply made it more possible, and acceptable, to express our intrinsic disposition?

Ask yourself: *What role (if any) does technology play in making me feel seen, known, or valued?* What is important is that we ponder our lives as they are now and consider whether we want to continue down this path. The next time you come home after buying grapes and feel inclined to immediately tweet your choice of red grapes over green, ask yourself, with curiosity, not judgment: *Why is it important to me that others know about this? If they know, does it change the experience of buying or eating these grapes? What changes or relaxes as a result of my making this experience known to the world?* And the next time you've spent a half hour reading posts about other people's trips to the grocery store, also ask yourself: *Am I truly interested in what I am reading? If not, why am I spending my time doing this?*

In this way we can use our need for constant visibility as an opportunity to understand ourselves better and to recognize how we are allowing technology to shape our lives. When we do this, we may make different decisions. Who knows? It may turn out that simply by bringing this kind of curious and kind attention to ourselves, our need for constant outside acknowledgment may ease. Or maybe we'll want to tweet to the world that we just spent the last ten minutes investigating our need to be seen, that we've officially become a more aware person. Regardless of how the inquiry impacts us, we will still have become more aware of ourselves and possibly of how we want to use our time and energy. Ultimately, awareness, whether it is tweeted or not, is still the path to freedom.

27

when becoming popular
is our purpose

Ayoung woman recently came to me feeling excited and proud of herself. When I asked why, she told me she had managed to acquire twenty new Instagram followers, cracking the ceiling she had previously been unable to crack. She had achieved this "accomplishment" by using her Instagram credits in a particular way that I didn't quite understand. While it was not clear if the new followers actually signed up themselves, she was quick to inform me that they were indeed real people, even though she didn't know them personally.

For many, this is the new definition of "accomplishment"—raising our number of followers on social media and thereby achieving the impression that we are interesting and, of course, popular. The importance of athletic, academic, artistic, and personal accomplishments is diminishing, while succeeding at getting our selfie a one-minute spot on Instagram's front page is increasingly a source of confidence and pride. In the digital age, "popular" is the identity and achievement to strive for, and being seen as cool is the new purpose of life!

Belonging is a basic human need. According to the pioneering psychologist Abraham Maslow, a sense of belonging ranks just after our primary needs of food, water, and physical safety. People have always wanted and needed to be included in the group, whatever the group may be. But belonging is not the same thing as being popular or likable as we now understand those terms. Now, many of us want to be popular for the sake of being popular, not because it means that we are personally well liked, honorable, or particularly good at anything.

Popularity has become a goal unto itself, an end result with no real larger meaning. Even after some of us have satisfied the basic need of establishing a healthy belonging in our lives, "popular" remains an identity we crave and chase, as we continually want to be assured that we are what other people like.

What's more, the so-called followers who create our popularity on social media are not actually followers in the true sense of the word. "Followers" used to mean people who believed in us and our ideas or values—devotees. Now followers are numbers we amass by using the Internet in increasingly clever ways. Often our followers know nothing about us or what it is they are supposedly following. The new follower is simply a statistic we buy when we "like" someone else's post or promote someone else's page. People even advertise: "If you follow me, I will follow you." The whole thing is a game of smoke and mirrors.

In even more extreme cases, followers are purchased that are not even real humans but web robots, otherwise known as bots. These followers don't exist at all, except as lines of computer code. The cat is out of the bag: you can buy followers! One website that sells virtual followers advertises that for just $3.00 you can add a thousand followers to your Twitter account.[1] For $379.99, another bookie in the popularity game will deliver fifty thousand new followers and, thus, instant popularity.[2] When you see a celebrity or someone else with an enormous number of followers, you can assume that some of those followers were probably purchased through a company that sells popularity. The absurdity is that then—this is where it gets really high-school-ish—other people follow that person because they think that person is popular. Just when you think it can't get any sillier, there's further to go: namely, some people follow these "popular" people even when they know that their followers aren't real! This leaves the emperor not only naked, but spanking mad!

There used to be a developmental stage in life, usually sometime in our thirties, when we shifted our focus from the outside to the inside. That is, we stopped defining ourselves by what others thought of us and became more interested in what we thought of ourselves and the world. This stage could be called "growing up." It seems that this stage of life is now disappearing for many of us. Now, the question *Do I like myself?* has been replaced by *Am I liked?*

Very young people run the Internet industry, and for that generation, popularity as a pursuit makes sense and is even appropriate to some degree. But as the Internet takes over more and more of our lives, those of us who are not creating code are taking on the values of the generation that drives the Internet. All great movements of change began because someone was willing to stand for something that wasn't popular. I wonder, do we still have the courage to put our names on something that has no followers? If it had always been the way it's become now, would any of the great revolutions ever have come to pass?

Is being popular really what we want to hold up as the most meaningful thing in life, the sign of real achievement? Because this is precisely what many of us are now modeling for our children. We are encouraging them to chase approval (no matter how approval comes about or how shallow or fleeting it is), and we are teaching them to determine their own worth by external sources (even if they don't know or respect some of the people following them). Can we wrestle back some kind of mature and thoughtful relationship with what we consider important, a relationship that has more substance and is more lasting than the number of "likes" we get on the Instagram photo of our mango margarita? "Likes" are flimsy planks on which to build a house of self-worth and moral structure. It seems to me that if we adults don't reestablish some sane gauge for what is valuable in life—what sustains and nourishes us, makes us feel genuinely well, and gives us a deeper sense of meaning—we will emotionally and spiritually bankrupt both ourselves and generations to come. We will certainly rob our children of the experience of true self-esteem.

What if one day there is no longer a private, internal self left to consult on what is important, and all that remains is a universal, Internet-based, computer-coded self to judge what is meaningful? As long as we are not yet bots ourselves, we still have time to put our precious attention on becoming people we respect, that is, on becoming our own destinations regardless of who or what else has gone viral.

Ask yourself now, *Do I like myself? Do I respect myself?* Notice where in your body you go looking for the answers. And then ask yourself, *What is my definition of accomplishment?* and *Who decides what I consider valuable and what life goals I pursue?*

The truth is, no matter how or for what we are living right now, if we are awake and aware, we can always take back ownership of our lives and reestablish what *we* consider valuable and what goals *we* want to pursue.

Ultimately, the best lesson we can relearn for ourselves and teach to the younger generations is that true and lasting cool has nothing to do with this moment's "virality." At the very least, to know this gives our children a chance at possessing real confidence; it gives them a shot at creating a life that will provide them with lasting substance. But we adults have to model this mindset first, assigning worth back where it belongs and not letting the Internet and social media determine our larger human priorities. The purpose we set for our lives shapes those lives, and certainly we want more than a life that has been shaped and guided by the whims of technopopularity. No matter how old you are, popularity as a raison d'être is not enough.

28

heads floating in cyberspace

Over and over I am asked this similar question: If I am present with technology, truly engaged in what I am doing on my device, paying close attention to whatever is on my screen, why does this not constitute being here in the moment? Can't technology be its own present moment, its own "now"? In truth, what appears on our screen is an object of attention, but to be truly present, we need more than just an object of attention and engagement with the thoughts that are currently arising.

When you say that *you* are here, present, who or what exactly is it that is present? What part of you needs to be here in order for you to say that *you* are here? If you are sitting on a park bench eating an apple, but your attention is lost in the story of thoughts firing in your mind, your body may be here physically, but you, your awareness, is not here. You are not aware of tasting that apple, hearing the birds, feeling the breeze, or noticing anything else happening in the space and time your body physically occupies. Where and what your body is living is not where and what your attention is living. You are not present in your current reality. As a result, you are not where *you* are. Presence requires that we be embodied and connected to our senses and that our attention be in sync with where our bodies are at this moment in time.

Thoughts are the primary seducers that pull our attention away from here, luring us out of the moment and separating us from where our bodies are actually living. When we are on technology, we are attentive to and present in a world that is not the same world our bodies are living in. As such, we can miss out, not only on the taste of that apple but on our whole lives.

The fact that people continue to ask me why technology isn't just a different kind of present moment or a new version of "now" suggests that both our identities and our sense of what *here* means are becoming virtual. We are coming to see ourselves, who we are, as heads floating in virtual space, attached to nothing except perhaps the pixels appearing on our screens. For far too many of us, our identities are no longer embodied. We have a digital identity to match our digital world. As a result, what our senses are experiencing (or would be experiencing if we were present) is becoming irrelevant—as is, for that matter, what is happening in real time in our physical reality. Being where we are has come to mean being where our minds are, whether or not that includes our bodies and a sensory-lived reality. Real time is being conflated with virtual time.

Why is it important to be present where our bodies are? Why is where the body is any more important or of the present moment than where the mind is? These questions are in some way unanswerable. But perhaps it comes down to an issue of identity: whom we believe we are and what we believe constitutes the present moment. To imagine ourselves to be just mind, just whatever thoughts and distractions our attention is drawn to at a particular moment, and to imagine *here* as just wherever our mind has taken us constitute a profoundly limited way of seeing who we are—and what a moment is made of. It's like believing we are stuck inside a fish tank when in fact that fish tank has no lid and is sitting in the middle of the sea.

What's more, when we are identified with mind and believe the present moment to be whatever thought we are paying attention to, most of the time we then experience great suffering. While entertaining and interesting at times, the mind's basic state is one of dissatisfaction and unrest; it is always looking to get to somewhere else. When we spend our days (and often nights too) off in the virtual ether, flitting from one mind activity to another, submerged in thoughts and distractions, we are living *in* our minds and *as* our minds. We are disembodied, disconnected from our senses, ungrounded, cut off from life as it is happening, and "twired," that is, simultaneously tired and wired. For most people, the mind is not a comfortable residence, much less a joyful place to inhabit.

On the other hand, when we sync up our attention and our senses and land where we actually are, a deep and palpable presence emerges, a wholeness that comes from experiencing our own life force, which doesn't flit about like the mind but rather remains steady and constant. When the body is inhabited, it tethers us to our earthboundedness, our rootedness, and this gives us the sense of being genuinely here in our lives. Put simply, we need to be present in our senses to feel present in our lives.

Working as a therapist for many years, I can say the following with 100 percent certainty: people feel more connected to themselves and to their lives, more aware and present, when they make their bodies their homes. The senses usher us into the moment, and they deliver us here with an immediacy that is reliable and profound. Mindfulness is the practice of learning to pay attention to and reside in our embodied reality, directly experiencing our senses in each moment. Mindfulness is the practice of presence. No matter how virtual life becomes or we become, this real-life body and its experience in physical time and space are still the doorway to our deepest well-being.

Right now, slowly, move your attention through the different parts of your body: face, hands, shoulders, chest, belly, legs, feet, and whatever else beckons. Invite each area to relax and soften. Rather than observing or noting what you feel, actually feel the sensations directly, from the inside out. Sense any warmth or tingling that your inner presence evokes. And now feel your whole body, here, where you are seated. Sense "hereness" itself. Feel the vibration of just being.

Stay with this physically felt sense of being for a minute or two. If you discover that you've drifted off and are lost in thought, no big deal—simply return your attention to one of your anchors: sound, breath, or body sensation. Simply come back into your body, into the senses, and into the feeling of presence itself. Enjoy being here.

29

uncovering our limitless self

spend a lot of time thinking about Generation V (for "Virtual"), the one that is growing up in a world where people are brands and we're all frantically running around announcing who we are, what we like and dislike, and what we stand for. I wonder how young people will develop in a world of virtual doppelgängers. I wonder how they will learn to connect who they are with something more fundamental and lasting than their last tweet, something deeper than just their online persona and the feedback it receives, something more essential than the information they can post about themselves on Facebook. In truth, I wonder about this not just for our youth but for all of us.

My younger daughter is at an age when she is continually proclaiming, "I am Gretchen." She has taken her name to be who she is. Her being and the word *Gretchen* are now one, inseparable. Soon she will begin adding to her list of "I ams": "I am . . . a girl, a sister, a daughter, a granddaughter, a friend, a student, a chocolate lover." And still later, she will perhaps *be* a particular profession, political party, sexual orientation, relationship status, psychological history, as well as *be* her memories, dreams, opinions, feelings, and personality. As we go on in life, the list of roles, things we stand for, accomplishments, ideas, and all the rest that we believe we are grows infinitely long.

The real issue with all of this identification, this creation of a "me," is that whatever we consider our "me" to be, it then has to be defended. We are not okay if our story of "me" is not okay. We must be on guard at all times against what is coming in from the world, always protecting our version of our self, making sure that it stays intact and that nothing and no one puts it in jeopardy. With each additional identity hat we put on and imagine our self to be, the "me," our being, the essence beneath the costume, becomes more obscured and constricted, as we become increasingly cut off from our fundamental vastness—our true self.

Thus far, as my daughter sees it, she *is* Gretchen—although just this week she did add to her idea of her self. This week, in her young mind, she became combined with "girlness." Now, as she understands it, she *is* a girl. Girlness is thus part of her basic essence, of who she is—actually, to be more accurate, she has taken on the identity of "a big girl," not just "a girl." But to be a name or a gender is not that burdensome because there isn't much to defend. If I am Jon and you are Ed, my identity and worth are not in danger as result of your having a different name. If I am a girl and you are a boy, I don't need to turn you into a girl to make my girlness valid or right. As time passes, however, and we become more entrenched in and identified with our ideas, opinions, relationships, emotional traumas, accomplishments, and roles—our story of "me"—life grows more dangerous, and our version of who we are requires that far more elements line up. We have so much more to defend than when we were just a name and a little or big gender.

If who I *am* is a "popular person" and then I post something that no one "likes," my very notion of my self is called into question, and thus I am not safe. If I can't be my story about my self, I can't be. Similarly, if who I *am* is a particular career and that career goes away, I feel that I go away. If I *am* my political opinions and I encounter someone with conflicting views, then I need to destroy their opinions to maintain my own sense of being. If my opinions are wrong in another person's eyes, then *I* am wrong, fundamentally, since I *am* my opinions. If I am a wife and the marriage ends, I have lost my self, ceased to be, because I can no longer play that role. If I define myself as my emotional trauma, then experiencing joy is a risk to who I am. When we believe ourselves to be our story about our self, then we are always in danger and always having to live in a self-protective way.

Technology is now the ultimate venue for defining ourselves by way of our attributes, encouraging us to lock ourselves into an identity, to proclaim "who we are." Every time we announce something about ourselves on social media or fill out an online profile, we add yet another item to the "I am [fill in the blank]" identity and dump yet another construct on top of our life-force. Every time we claim "the kind of person we are" and contract ourselves into that definition, we shrink ourselves into a finite form.

With so much to protect and defend, it becomes impossible to be open to what life is presenting from moment to moment, to meet life freshly and let it be what it is. As a result, life becomes very small, and our responses to life are fear driven. We cannot see things as they really are but only in terms of whether what is coming in supports or threatens our story of who we are, what we call "me." Life then shrinks down to something we merely get through, with the hope that our "me" will be intact when it goes into the ground. Our fixed and fragile identities ultimately create a life of suffering and limitation.

In truth, we are like the ocean that takes the particular shape of a wave for a short time. But we forget our oceanness and believe ourselves to be just the wave. We are pure infinite presence before conditioning locks us into a small and separate person. We are free before we become captive to our story and mired in the responsibilities of defending our personhood. We are simply "I am" before we become "I am . . . everything else," all of which changes and passes, like the ocean waves. The remarkable thing is that we can reclaim this freedom, this knowing, and surrender our story of "me" while we are still living. Liberation, relief, and joy bubble over when we realize we don't have to be that person we keep describing and defending. As a result, we can finally just *be* in life, knowing that fundamentally we are not any of the hats we wear and that we are infinitely larger than any story we tell about who we are.

You might ask, *Do we need to know ourselves as the sum of our hats before we can take them off and realize our self as that which is hatless? Must we believe that we are the wave before we can realize our self as the ocean? Do we need to be a somebody before we can be liberated into being a nobody?* Perhaps. To maintain a sense of equanimity and well-being in this new world of Internet-created, branded identities, we certainly need to be able to appreciate our individuality—the experiences, thoughts, feelings, talents, preferences, histories, and everything else that describe us. They're all true. But at the same time, we can retain a sense of our self as that primary being that precedes all conditioning, as that presence which does not depend upon anything *about* us.

Particularly now, in the age of virtual identity, when selves are created and destroyed in 140-character bundles, it is important to discover a sense of our true identity, presence itself, free from all the labels that need defending. It is important to know that there is an I that simply is—not that is a something, but that just is. A connection to our vastness—to the being that was there before we became a somebody with a story and an Instagram account—will ultimately protect us from the fragile identity generating and identity defending that make life feel so perilous and small these days.

Pointing ourselves toward our fundamental "I-am-ness," the life-force that we are and were before we became a story, is like following a path of bread crumbs that leads us to come home to ourselves. Chances are we will have to travel through and shed a considerable number of "I-am-this-or-thats" along the way. But no matter how many years we've lived, it is wise to invite ourselves into the presence that is behind all our labels, behind the branding of the self that is now a requirement. In this way, we are preparing ourselves to remember—and know—our true self, our fundamental essence, which is infinite, indestructible, and irrevocable.

PART
4

creating space—
inside and out

30

finding silence inside the noise

Peter, a client, travels the world with one specific purpose: to find a place where the noise stops. Far and wide, he searches for one thing, silence. These days, rings, dings, alerts, alarms, one-sided cell phone conversations, and just plain noise follow us everywhere. Sometimes the noise makes us feel like we are going to go mad, because there is literally nowhere to find relief from the relentless cacophony of technology.

In many cities, even when we get in a taxicab—a space that used to be a bubble of quiet, sealed away by ourselves—we are now bombarded by noise coming off a screen a few inches away from our faces, a screen that we generally cannot turn off no matter what button we frantically jab. When we wait at the airport, we now must endure dozens of screens above our heads, spewing out information we don't want or need. Bars and restaurants, too, even those that are supposed to be intimate, have now fallen victim to the same din, with screens that invade the space transmitting voices that clamor for our attention. We live in what feels like an intensive care unit, with no break from the constant racket of technology. Unfortunately, the care that we are receiving is not serving us—it is not what we actually need in order to be well.

Not surprisingly, researchers are discovering that the more technology-induced noise we are bombarded with, the less we trust or can bear silence.[1] It seems we start believing we need the noise to be okay, afraid of what will happen when the noise stops and we're left alone in the quiet.[2] We are afraid that there will be nothing, that we will be nothing inside the silence.

Just as our ears are slammed with external noise, each moment inside our minds is jammed with internal noise. Our minds are teeming with bells, chimes, and train whistles of their own sort as the presence of technology stimulates the activity inside our heads—more thoughts, more commentary, more chatter, more information, more entertainment, more everything, all of which is supposed to be a good thing.

We live in a society whose members constantly move from one object of attention to the next, afraid there might be a momentary gap, a silence or a space between the objects of attention, which would leave us nowhere, in dead space, without something to interact with. We avoid silence because we view it as unfamiliar and threatening. We view it, not as a sound of its own, but rather as an emptiness or a lack, a space devoid of substance, in which we feel our own unsupplemented being. Like a fetus that cannot survive without its mother's umbilical cord, we are unable to maintain a sense of being without a feeding tube to something else.

But deep in our hearts, if we could get quiet enough to hear its whispers, lives the relief from the inner and outer noise that we long for. Some part of us always aches to come home to ourselves, to that place of serenity that is always awaiting us beneath the racket of life. In the same way that we long for silence, we also ache for space, for room to breathe and relief from the internal and external clutter. We crave the experience of spaciousness, of open sky, a place where we can escape the trap of all the stuff in both our digital and digitally infused mental worlds. We know what we need, and it is not more stuff or more noise.

Space is not just the absence of stuff, and silence is not just the absence of noise. Silence is its own profoundly important experience. It gives us the opportunity to process what we are living through, to hear our own thoughts and feelings, to notice and be mindful of our inner and outer worlds. Through the doorway of silence, we find true rest, a place where we can stop having to generate something or to pay attention to anything external. Listening to and residing in silence, we discover a place of simply being and can experience our own presence, which is entirely fulfilling in its own right. Unlike the demands that noise always includes, we discover that the presence silence offers us takes no effort. Presence is what is here when all the effort stops. This presence is what we truly are, under all the noise and clutter. Silence is our essence.

Introducing silence into our lives is a profound gesture of self-care, an invitation and an opportunity to spend time with ourselves, to remember ourselves as what we truly are. We can begin to bring silence into our lives in small ways by simply setting aside a bit of time every day to turn off the noise of technology and be quiet, listening to what remains when the noise is removed. As well, we can set aside time to be in a quiet environment, to inhabit places where we can hear the sound of silence, and our own being, without interruption. Small efforts to deliberately create quiet in our lives are powerful and transforming.

This can only happen, however, when we acknowledge the importance of silence and notice the profound relief it brings to our being. Although we are not conditioned to revere silence in this society or to know it as something that the human mind, body, and spirit actually require, nonetheless, with awareness, we can regain this understanding and respect for silence. Once we start to taste its effects and know it as a real place, an entity unto itself, with its own sound and qualities, we will crave silence more and more. We will become aware of our deep need for it and give ourselves permission to honor that need. When we come to understand silence as something that our basic well-being depends upon, something that we also deeply want, we will discover that it is always available to us, even in the cacophony of our digital world.

We can find silence when we commit to finding it, whether that search takes us into a bathroom stall or a meditation hall. Silence is always available to us in our internal world as well, when we tune into our own presence and make listening to inner silence our practice. Our being is silent by nature. We have filled it with noise, but if we choose to, we can always listen to what is under the noise. And with all the technological noise surrounding us, we need and deserve to give ourselves silence now more than ever.

making time for downtime

A woman I know is afraid to go to bed at night. She's not afraid of the dark or of having a nightmare. She's not afraid of someone breaking into her apartment or of dying in her sleep. What she's afraid of is the unfocused downtime that bedtime brings, the time when she is not attending to anything specific, accomplishing a task, or focused on something external. She's afraid of open time with herself.

Someone else I know described the experience of lying in bed one morning without any particular task to get up for and simultaneously not being able "to find" anything to think about. He said he felt like he had nowhere "to put his mind" and, as a result, like he was going insane. The absence of a focus for his attention sent him into a full-fledged panic attack.

These scenarios may sound strange, but they are more common than you might imagine. With the advent of the digital age, our attention is perpetually focused on something. We are playing a game, texting, researching, watching, or talking—always *doing*—our minds turned toward and engaged with something outside of ourselves. We treat our undirected attention the way a parent might treat a toddler on a long plane ride, frantically shoving activities and videos in front of their face until either the child passes out or the ride comes to an end.

Today many of us share this same fear of our own unentertained adult minds.

The gap, the space between activities, or what we used to call downtime, is disappearing from our lives. With our attention almost always narrowed onto an activity, we are losing the spaces in which our attention is open, without a specific focus. Some people say we are becoming unfocused as a society, but in fact we are becoming hyper-focused, always looking *at* something and never just looking, without a specific object or goal for our gazes.

Open awareness, downtime, the gap—whatever you call it—serves an important purpose in our lives. When I have a problem I can't solve, I will often go for a walk and drop thinking about the problem altogether. Later that day, after I've not thought about it for some time, the solution generally appears in my mind. I am not unique in having this experience. Something is actually happening in that downtime. The subconscious is putting things together, making associations, and doing a different kind of work, which happens outside our awareness.[1] For many people, it is in these gaps that they have their best flashes of insight, as if we need to take our minds *off* of something in order to gain access to our intuition—and, really, to our deepest wisdom.[2]

Like a child, the mind needs recess periods in its day, when it can just run and play, jump from thing to thing and not have to narrow its attention onto any particular object or event. The mind needs to be able to flow freely from thought to thought or simply to rest in no thought with an open and diffuse focus. Downtime between tasks allows our minds to rest, and this lowers our stress levels.[3] Gaps in the day give us time to just float about, space out, or take much-needed breaks from mental activity. They allow us to reboot our systems and come back to our tasks refreshed and attentive. When our attention is narrowly focused on something all the time, we become mentally exhausted, and though more time is spent focusing on tasks, we in fact become qualitatively less productive.[4]

What's more, when we're not playing a game or engaged in a Google search, we can hear our own thoughts and feelings, contemplate our experience, check in, and discover how we are doing in the middle of all this modern life. Having our attention constantly focused on technology disables our ability to focus on ourselves.

And yet the media tells us that we are focusing on ourselves more than ever, becoming pathological narcissists. The millennials, the generation born between the 1980s and 1990s, have even been dubbed

"Generation Me" by the media.[5] We are spending far more time than ever before reporting on ourselves, who we are, where we've been, and what we are doing, but that also means we are spending far less time actually *being* with ourselves, inside our own attention, inquiring and investigating our own experiences. Sadly, as a result of always relentlessly having an external focus, we have come to view the space of being with ourselves, undistracted, as a panic-inducing nonplace—a void.

From a spiritual perspective, the spaces between—between tasks, between thoughts, between breaths, between all the objects of our attention—are profoundly important. Such is the space we inhabit during meditation. It is in the spaces between thoughts that we connect with the awareness within which thought happens. In this open awareness we gain a sense of detachment and freedom from the mind. When we lose the ability to live in the gaps, we become slaves to the mind, terrified of any moment when the mind is not occupied. Gaps then become a kind of death, as if we cease to exist when they occur. On the other hand, when we can tolerate and even enjoy open, undirected space, when being with just ourselves is not something to be feared, a deep and lasting confidence arises.

Breaks from focused attention are beneficial in myriad ways. They bring insight, allow us to solve problems without trying, and give our minds a chance to rest and to play. When they are experienced mindfully, gaps allow us time to spend with ourselves, to experience our own being, and to know ourselves as more than just what we are doing and thinking. Such gaps strengthen our ability to stop trying to outrun open space, escape downtime, and ultimately dodge ourselves.

In the digital age we value information and entertainment, the stuff that fills the gaps, and we are encouraged to keep the mind busy, engaged, or just plain distracted at all times. If we want downtime, we have to actively create the space for that to happen. Ironically, creating space in which we can be unfocused now takes focused attention.

On a practical level, we can begin to create downtime in small ways. For example, we can take five minutes every day to consciously resist the urge to give our minds something to chew on. When our minds tell us it's time to play a game, email a friend, research a vacation, figure out a work problem, or write a to-do list, we can just say, "No, not now." Although the mind will always search for something to attend to, we can practice being aware without having to direct our awareness *at* something. Try it in short stretches and notice what unfolds, whether you feel different. Or, similarly, take a walk without your phone or any other device and let your mind just wander. Set aside times for an approved "space out." Give yourself the gift of the gap, the privilege that used to be built into life but no longer is.

As a result, not only might you feel less mentally fatigued, you may also discover a sense of internal spaciousness, a wider and more panoramic view of life than you normally experience, one that is not frantic and does not depend on external material to enable you to escape an internal void. With enough practice, your own presence may become a place unto itself, and you may discover that it is in the spaces between your objects of attention that you feel most calm, whole, and, ultimately, well.

32

creating meaning amid
the meaninglessness

attended Friday-night services at synagogue recently, and throughout the week that followed I was aware of feeling profoundly
human, grounded, and complete, part of the world. As is custom-
ary, the evening services included singing, meditation, and a talk from
the rabbi. Although the topic of the talk changes weekly, its universal
theme is constant—namely, the experience of being human. The evening I attended, the talk was about our relationship with obstacles and
fear. We addressed our human desire to run from what scares us and
were counseled to lean into our fears and work with our limitations,
not against them. That wise counsel is particularly applicable to this
time in history, when our devices and the limitless distractions they
offer provide us with infinite ways to escape our fears and, really, all
unwanted experience.

The in-house services and deep contemplation that this rabbi and
countless spiritual leaders offer each week are important not only
because of the messages they deliver but also because of their power
to make us feel connected to something vaster than our ever-changing
personal experience. They provide a narrative for our lives, mark the
stages and passages of life, place us in a larger and more profound
human context, and address the myriad shared aspects of this mortal
journey. Services provide bones for the body of life. We come to understand that we are living something that is part of a larger story and that
it is deserving of our most serious attention.

Given the fact that we as a society, and particularly our younger
generations, are spending far more time than ever before engaged in

the shallow banter of social media, I am wondering how this shift will impact us in the long run. What I see in my psychotherapy practice is that people feel increasingly disconnected from a sense of context, meaning, and the greater human narrative. They speak of being untethered and not knowing what their lives are supposed to be about or even when they are going to begin. The teen years disappear into the twenties and then the thirties and onward, while people wait to feel connected to some purpose or permanence, something bigger and more lasting than their momentary dramas, pleasures, and irritations. They imagine their real lives will one day have the weight that real life is supposed to carry. Along with this, there is a growing sense of ungroundedness or placelessness in people's experience, as if the larger narrative within which their lives once made sense is slipping away.

Social media is about immediacy. Even the word *media* is built into *immediacy*. In social media, before you can finish a thought there is a new one to replace it: *I am drinking a latte. I like this movie. I hate this steak. I disagree with this decision* . . . ad infinitum. Immediacy itself is not the problem. Rather, indulging in posting every thought that passes through our consciousness, without considering whether it offers anything of meaning to the world, discourages critical and mature thinking. The ceaseless bombardment of irrelevant content creates an environment of shallowness. Instant and trivial is how it is—the opposite of deep contemplation. Social media can leave us feeling like we are missing a larger context in which to place our human story. Our own journey, indeed our own being, can come to feel as transitory and meaningless as the latest tweet.

It is important to come together shoulder to shoulder to contemplate life, to consider where we fit into the larger human story and what meaning our individual and collective journeys hold. It is important that we give weight to this thing called existence, to our place in time. This contemplative process not only keeps us feeling well but also tethers us to the earth at a time when we feel floating and lost. We mature when we examine our place and purpose on earth, and we develop wisdom and substance, which also help to ground us. In acknowledging and considering our shared experience as human beings, we grow more connected to others, ourselves, and the world at large. We deepen our experience of life as we honor that which is not purely pleasurable and ephemeral.

As we dive ever more deeply into the world of technology and social media, we need to pay attention to the quality and depth of the content we're sharing and receiving. In our love affair with the instantaneous, we can still choose to maintain the discipline that allows us to feel our roots, the ground beneath our feet, and all that has come before us and will come after our momentary musings have disappeared from the Twitter feed. We cannot maintain a sense of meaning or wholeness in a world made entirely of pixels. Then we become pixels ourselves, without a sense of where we are or even *if* we are. It is crucial that we make the effort to move beyond immediate distraction and entertainment and consciously bring the larger picture, of which we are part, into our lives.

In order to correct the conditions of ungroundedness and disconnection that are now epidemic, we need to consciously spend time contemplating meaning, our humanness in this digital world. One thing is for sure: ground and meaning are not pop-ups that will magically appear within us while we're clicking between Pinterest and Facebook. We need to create a real-life practice—a time for contemplation or meditation built into every day (even five minutes)—to address our deeper needs for meaning and purpose, and we need to treat such needs with a quality of attention that matches their profound importance in our lives. Simply put, contemplating meaning gives rise to meaning.

33

discovering being
in a doing world

We are a society of doers. We are always thinking: *What can I do? What should I do?* And the double "do": *What do I do?* When you suggest to people that they stop trying to do something, just for a moment, often they grow anxious and sometimes even angry. In response, they usually get busy doing something else right away. It seems we can't just sit back and do nothing, just be where we are. We need to be doing something and, most importantly, moving forward. Indeed, moving forward is, for many, the purpose of life. But while setting goals can create positive motivation and direction, goals can also interfere with being present now and appreciating what's here—before the goal has been reached.

We are conditioned to believe that in order to live an important and full life, we must have a purpose. We are supposed to have something we want to get done. We should wake up in the morning with a clear idea of what we are working toward. Indeed, many people feel lost and depressed when they don't have a purpose, as if their lives have no meaning and they themselves are failures. "Purposeless" essentially means useless. We believe that if we are not heading somewhere, we are nowhere. We also believe it is our fault when we don't have a purpose and therefore it is something we need to remedy, sooner rather than later. A life without a purpose is not considered a life at all.

Many yoga classes begin with the teacher asking the students to set an intention for their practice. Students are asked "to make a plan" for what they want to get out of the time they're about to spend on the mat, to identify "a goal" for what they want their practice to do for them. They are encouraged to decide how they want the next ninety minutes to change their "now." Even when we are practicing being present, many of us still need to be heading somewhere else. Much of self-help today is about clarifying what we want to do with our lives, learning to make maps for our life plans, and then figuring out what we need to do to make those plans happen. Almost everywhere we look, we are being asked to do something to make "now" something better than just . . . now.

What is my purpose? Where am I going? It is the mind that asks these questions and the mind that answers them. Paradoxically, we have assigned the perpetrator of our suffering the task of curing our suffering. Our what-do-we-do-now conditioning, ironically, excludes "now." This would be more accurately expressed as, "What do we do about now?" Such a mindset inspires an antagonistic relationship with the present moment. We believe that there is always a better place to get to, a better experience to be found than what we are living right now. And chances are that "better" can be found on or through technology. How could this moment ever measure up to what else is possible, when everything else is possible right here in our palms?

Technology makes it easy to just keep moving from one titillating experience to another, never having to come back here to be with "just" ourselves, "just" now. "What else is there?" has become our societal mantra, replacing "What's here?" as the question of the day. With technology at the center of our lives, it's no longer necessary to inhabit the present moment—it's not even necessary to notice the basic restlessness and discomfort that the present moment includes.

The more we chase after a better next moment, the more firm our belief grows that the lacking nature of the present moment is the culprit of our restlessness. Technology not only provides us with the ideal means by which to disappear from the moment but also simultaneously allows us to blame the moment itself and its inadequacy for our disappearance—the perfect device.

The secret to being well completely contradicts what we have been taught. Well-being happens when we stop trying to figure out what we need to do to get to a better future. Ironically, equanimity appears when we live without a future, without a "next," and without an intention or a purpose for what this moment and this life should become. Well-being happens when we move from becoming to being.

How utterly radical it is to live *without* intention, and how utterly freeing it is. But be prepared: the mind will scream in protest when you drop "What do I do?" as your life's mantra. *But my life will never be what I want and nothing will ever happen if I don't do something to make it happen!* No matter what your mind screams, though, take a chance, be courageous, give it a whirl, and see what you discover. If the experiment fails, you can always return to your intentions and agendas and the experts who will be there waiting to help you figure out what you need to do about your life.

In truth, life actually happens when you *stop* doing something with it and to it. But to trust this fact, you have to discover it for yourself. When you live with here as your destination, life gets better and much easier. You can relax and become part of the natural unfolding of life, the process you think you are making happen. When you stop asking, "What do I do?" and start asking, "What's here, now?" you discover that the presence you are after, the place of no effort, is right here, without your having to do anything at all. Trust that life, as its own force, doesn't need you to force it forward.

34

getting the importance
of not getting

Every December I attend the last church service of the year, during which the minister asks us to write down all the things we want for the coming year. We draft a letter in which we thank the universe for giving us the things on our list, and a year later it is sent back to us by the church. We write down what we want, decide we are going to get it, and adopt the gratitude that comes with already having it. "Thank you for the new job that I love." "Thank you for helping my family get along." "Thank you for selling my home at the right price."

Three weeks ago I received the letter I wrote last December. As always, it's interesting to read what was important to me a year ago and, of course, to see what did and didn't come to fruition. This year, out of a list of twenty-seven things, three and a half came to be. About fifteen no longer mattered to me, and there were eight and a half things that I still want but have not yet been able to manifest. The same numbers would probably hold if I had not written the letter, but it's a useful exercise nonetheless. As I looked over my list, I was struck with a different kind of gratitude than I usually feel when I read my letter from myself. While I was of course grateful for what I did get and what did happen, this time I realized that, oddly, I was more grateful for what I didn't get and for what had come to me as a result of not getting what I wanted.

Because of what the universe had so kindly denied me, I was forced to grow in ways I could never have imagined. I might have wished for the growth, but I never would have chosen the path by which the growth came—the path through which I learned my most important lessons. By not getting something that was on my list, for example, I was pushed to find out why I felt I needed that particular thing and the experience I believed that thing would bring to my life. In other words, I was able to discover what I was really craving. As a result of not getting what I wanted, I was able to address the emotional nourishment I actually needed and provide it for myself in ways that would not have been possible had I received the actual thing I asked for. In another example, by not getting what I wanted, I was able to realize that I really did not need it at all, that I was okay without it, and to let go of a long-held belief that I could not do without this particular thing. Overall, I learned that I was far stronger than I had thought and that I was indeed whole, with or without my desired things.

In addition to the lessons we get to learn, having to do without forces us into the lucky experience of absence. "Who would want more absence?" you might ask. Technology creates the illusion, with our participation, that we can and should get more, and it should be better and come faster than what we currently have. In this digital environment, absence certainly doesn't sound like a prize. But the beauty of absence is that it provides us with the opportunity to meet ourselves. Again, this concept is a hard sell in a virtual world, where being with ourselves is not considered nearly as fulfilling as a game of Candy Crush. And yet doing without opens the door to discovering who we are underneath our cravings for all those things we want.

When the noise quiets—which in a virtual world is not something that naturally happens but a choice we have to consciously make—we can then meet who's listening in the silence, who is here to get or not get those desired things. Ironically, when we don't get the things we want, we are offered the gift of experiencing our own presence, our human-being-ness. In truth, as the teachings of the East often remind us, we don't need anything in order to be well and to experience peace. But to be unwell always requires something.

In the end, what we call "getting" so often does not come from getting in the way we think of it. We may not have gotten what we thought we wanted, but instead we got the opportunity to become a new person, a person we never would have become had we gotten what we wanted.

The next time you think about what you have received and what more you can get, investigate what is really true, beyond your checklist of things. We are trained to be grateful for getting the things we want, but we can and need to become equally grateful for the things that we don't get and the wonderful and unexpected opportunities and gifts that those absences bestow upon us—the presents and presence that we could never have seen coming.

PART 5

how to liberate
ourselves from
a teched-out mind

35

overthrowing the
dictatorship of the mind

n the Buddhist tradition there is a saying that the mind is like a wild monkey that's locked in a cage, drunk a bottle of wine, and been stung by a bee. If that's what the mind was like before technology, then on technology the mind is a wild, locked-up monkey that's drunk two bottles of wine chased by a shot of Scotch and been stung by a whole swarm of bees.

If you pay attention to the way you feel after you've spent an entire day on technology, you'll know without any doubt that it has affected you. I've heard the feeling described as edgy, agitated, sick, empty, amped up, depleted, anxious, deadened, unfocused, burned out, depressed, scattered, jumpy, and irritable, among other things, but, in general, people do not describe a positive feeling. Technology turns the world into a cruise-ship buffet of information, one that never closes, and we are bingeing on this banquet, making ourselves sick with nonstop ingestion of too much information. Even though I am someone who spends a lot of time trying to understand the mind and the side effects of our digital drugs, I too am peppered with thoughts throughout the day about what I could do, find out, or check right now on my computer. What changes when we have more awareness is not necessarily that the thoughts stop but that responding to them becomes a choice and not a compulsion. This is awareness at work.

The digital age is to the human mind (the wild monkey) what the age of debauchery was to the human id. Technology, the way we are using it, is both intensifying the mind's busyness and honing its ability to create and maintain busyness. Technology is building those ungrounded aspects of mind that disrupt our basic equanimity and peacefulness. Jacked up on information, images, games, communication, and all the other stuff technology provides, our minds have become impulsive and insatiable beasts demanding to be fed continuously. When the mind suddenly wants to research travel deals at midnight, or track down the perfect lawn mower, or understand the intersection between strawberries and quantum physics, we, the stooge behind that mind, will get up out of bed to do it. We are the lackeys running behind the mind, serving its every whim and desire 24/7.

As the monkey mind grows stronger and more powerful inside us, it becomes harder to observe the mind itself and the thoughts it generates, harder to ground it in our deeper wisdom and sanity. The more the mind devours, the more it reinforces its own power, convincing us that it's good for us to be so stuffed, busy, and distracted all the time. As this process escalates, the room for discernment on our part diminishes. How we, who are listening to the thoughts, actually feel about the mind's dictatorship and who we are underneath all its chatter eventually become irrelevant. We simply give the mind more of what it wants, tossing it another app, another game, more mental snacks to chew on. We disappear a little more, while the monkey grows wilder and ever more powerful.

To ground our monkey mind and tether it to discernment, sanity, and wisdom, we must first become aware of what our mind is up to. We need to be mindful of the mind, listen carefully to what it's telling us *without assuming it knows what it's talking about*. It is important to turn our attention to the source of our internal movie rather than just surrendering into it, as if we have no choice. Awareness (without mental thought) is that energy of attention, a neutral witness, the presence that separates us from the mind's tsunami of thoughts, desires, and demands and our susceptibility to believing them. Awareness is the larger intelligence that can hear the mind but not identify with it, and in that capacity, awareness is our protector and liberator. We investigate the mind and the thoughts it creates from this place of awareness and as awareness itself. Knowing ourselves to be this awareness, we are protected from having to live as slaves under the mind's rule—and, ultimately, we are protected from the suffering that the mind itself, and the belief that we are the mind, creates.

36

how to stop narrating
and start being life

A monkey mind well fed on a diet of texting, tweeting, Face-booking, Snapchatting, and all sorts of other tasty tech-ing makes for a noisy, anxious, and relentless thinking machine. The more we use technology to saturate our minds with chatter, the more chatter our minds generate. If we listen to the contents of our noisy mind, in addition to the list of things wrong with us (and everyone else), what we're lacking, and the problems we need to solve, most of us will find that our inner chatter also contains a running description of the experience we are living right now. That is to say, we are continually telling ourselves the story of our lives, narrating the play by play of our existence.

One client explained to me that his mind never stops talking to him and about him, as if he were a character in his own self-written, self-directed, self-starring movie: *Hey you, me, look at what you're doing now. You're really enjoying this moment. Notice how well this interaction is going for you. They think you're terrific!* And on it goes.

The thought voiceover is a natural aspect of our minds, but technology provides us with a new vehicle, a Ferrari of sorts, with which to put this voiceover into accelerated action. Social media, texting, and other technologies all offer us both a publisher and an audience for our "me" story, a place to broadcast our narrative, which then supports and encourages us to keep the narration and chatter going, both inside our minds and on the screen.

Usually, our internal narrator describes not only what is happening but also our opinions about it, an incessant commentary on our experience: *I like this. I don't like this. I am interested in this. I am offended. This is a great thing. This is a terrible thing.* Why do we describe what is happening as it is happening? Aren't we already there, in the experience? Ask yourself, *Who is doing the narrating?* And perhaps even more importantly, *To whom is the narrator speaking?*

Sometimes we package our experience to prepare it for presentation. We put together the report on our life as it is happening so that we can know ahead of time how we will convey it to others. So, too, we continually explain our life to ourselves as a way to avoid directly feeling it, keeping it at arm's length so that it can't hurt us. We go straight to the description of our experience before we even allow ourselves to have the experience, good or bad. The secondhand story then becomes our life and what we get to feel. In this way, our internal narrator blocks us from getting to actually be in our life.

The mind believes we are the mind—all mind and nothing more. The mind needs to be able to tell us that we are here, or it thinks we won't be here anymore. The mind believes that if it stopped its running commentary and instead just let us experience our lives directly, without telling ourselves what we are experiencing, then the mind would no longer be needed, and it—or, more accurately, we—would cease to exist. Disappearing into life means, to the mind, disappearing altogether. The mind doesn't believe that there can be an experience of life unless the mind tells us about it. In its role as reporter, the mind is really in a fight for its own existence.

What's more, the mind narrates our experience in order to secure its position as our identity. As long as the mind is in charge of our life's voiceover, the experience belongs to the mind. It tells us how life is going for us, how we are doing in life. Like someone living in a country where the government controls the information, we end up experiencing life through the propaganda the mind doles out. Our direct experience is kidnapped by the mind. What it tells us is all that we get to experience. And at the same time that it controls our experience, the strong presence of the mind also keeps us identified with mind, such that we're not even aware of what we're missing out on. We end up with a self that is separate from what we're living. Imprisoned in this way, we're prevented from becoming fully immersed in and one with life. We sit passively on the shore, never getting to dive into the ocean.

In today's culture, we've become obsessed with the idea of being present. But what does it really mean to be present? What most people consider "being present" is being able to describe to ourselves what is happening in the moment. To be awake enough to notice and describe what is happening in the moment is indeed an accomplishment, but there is something far more wondrous and magical than just being able to describe experience!

What if you didn't have to live your life one step removed, as "the noticer," with the mind as your witness? What if you could live it directly, without any narration and commentary? Imagine how revolutionary: to live your life, be in your life, as it is unfolding, without constantly having to hear about it in your head. What if you could just be who you are without having to hear about who you are?

You can live this way, completely free from the "I" documentary the mind produces from moment to moment. Although it may never have occurred to you that you could live another way, you are not a hostage to your internal narrator. You can fire your narrator right now, without two weeks' notice! Once you become aware of the narrator's presence, you can set yourself free and drop the voiceover. I promise you, you will survive without the narrator. Who you survive as may change, but survive you will, in a new and fresh existence.

Stop listening when your mind tells you what is happening in the moment, what it thinks about it, and what that says about who you are. Turn away from the commentary and sense what you are actually experiencing. When you hear the narrator return with another story about your present moment, which it will, turn away again. Say, *No. Not interested. Leave me alone so I can be in my life for real.* Keep breaking the narration habit until the habit is broken. This doesn't happen overnight, so don't judge yourself for continuing to be distracted by your inner commentator. Be persistent in your determination to break this life habit. Notice what remains whenever the internal voiceover temporarily goes silent, when there is nothing left to separate you from life. Smell, taste, hear, see, touch, sense, feel, and be life. Dive in. No matter how powerful a particular experience may be from the narrator's point of view, the narrative cannot match what it is to be inside the experience itself.

We have made a science and indeed a multimillion-dollar industry out of figuring out how to be here now. But in truth, we cannot and do not need to *do* "being present." Quite the contrary. We cannot *not* be here in the present. It is our original and organic state. We are always here, and it is always this now. Everything else is an idea. In its constant narration of this moment, the mind makes "now" and "who you are" into two separate entities, when in fact there is only one. Stop telling yourself about your life, and in an instant, you will be off the shore and in the ocean—you and life will be one.

37

getting off the thought treadmill

f you stop for just a minute, right now, and pay attention to what you are hearing in your head, or what feels like your head, you will notice all sorts of disjointed and random thoughts. In the last minute, I'm aware of having had at least twenty: a memory of my mother's sneakers on visiting day at camp thirty-something years ago, the feel of the indoor arena beneath my boots at a horse show in the late nineties, something I need to tell my husband, dinner plans, fixing the piano, and, and, and . . . I won't bore you with the full list. Between such identifiable thoughts exists a background buzz, loud and energetic but without any specific content.

There is no reason or sense to how, when, and why thoughts appear. Thoughts simply appear without asking us if we want to listen to them. Still, we believe that we are the thinker of the thoughts we hear. Despite all evidence to the contrary, we think we decide what thoughts to think, and as a result, we think we are responsible for their content. Because they are "our" thoughts and we "did" the thinking, our identity is determined by the content of our thoughts. We are a good person if we have "good" thoughts and a bad person if we have "bad" thoughts. We spend a lot of time trying to control our thoughts and create order out of the chaos that the mind generates.

In truth, thoughts happen on their own. We are not in charge of what our thoughts are about. We are their recipients, the hearers of thoughts, the screens upon which they are projected, but we are not the generators of all those thoughts. We can make use of thoughts, but without needing them to be ours in some fundamental, identity-defining way. If you're like most people, much of what your mind tells you is material you've already heard before, many times. So, too, many of the thoughts you receive are useless or unremarkable. Only a small percentage might actually be of interest to you. Most of what we hear in our heads is mere chatter that wouldn't be missed if it weren't heard.

Technology actually encourages us to tune into our thoughts more closely, to honor them with even greater reverence. It used to be we could have hundreds of interesting, funny, delightful thoughts in a day that we alone enjoyed, and there was nothing to be done with them, no easy way of immediately making anyone else aware of them. Nowadays, with texting and tweeting and the many other astounding opportunities to transmit every moment inside our minds, we are paying closer attention to each piece of rubbish that floats by in the constant thought stream. We have a funny thought, and then we tweet it; a clever remark, and we text it; a question about something we see on the street, and we Wikipedia it; a fancy for a chocolate recipe, and we Google it; a question about how to get the red wine we spilled out of the suede pillow, and we Ask Jeeves for advice. Everything is heard, heeded, and responded to. This is a tremendous burden that often drains much of our energy.

What if we didn't have to take credit, blame, or responsibility for the appearance of our thoughts? What if we could make use of thought or not, but without viewing ourselves as the creator of all our thoughts? What if we didn't have to do anything about or with the thoughts the mind produces? What if we could just let them happen? Indeed, all this is possible! The fact is that the mind is kind of a crazy place sometimes, and for no understandable reason, wild and strange thoughts appear to everyone, thoughts that are out of sync with anything we believe or would ever actually do. How liberating it is to be given permission to let the mind do its thing without our having to take any action at all or mistake our thoughts for our identity.

Try this for a day: Let your mind fire off like the unchecked computer it is. Don't get involved in the contents of what it fires. Don't feed its firings with your attention or build a storyline from its random fragments. Don't do anything with the thoughts; instead, starve them of your attention—be careful, however, not to turn this instruction into another thought that engages you. Let thoughts simply pass through, like weather, and get on with your life. Imagine yourself inside a giant mosquito net with hundreds of mosquitoes buzzing just outside the net, unable to get through. You can ignore the mosquitoes and go about your business without getting bitten. And when not paid attention to, mosquitoes often take off to find someone else to bite. The same is true of our thoughts: without our energy, our blood, in the form of attention, they don't gain power. We can't stop having thoughts, but we can stop being so interested in and controlled by them—that is, we can stop taking our thoughts so personally.

The you who is hearing the thoughts *is* who you are. You are the space within which thoughts appear and disappear. Practice letting thoughts happen and turning away from them, and then notice what is there in the silence behind the noise. Indeed, you may find that by starving the mind in this way, you provide yourself with the most profound form of nourishment. The mind is not yours to control. Let the mind do its thing—while you do yours!

38

our thoughts are not real

f you imagine thoughts as birds flying in the sky of our awareness, we humans tend to jump on the back of whichever bird appears and ride it without question. Many of us don't know that we can decide which thoughts we want to engage, which rides we want to take. Instead, we just assume that if a thought appears, we must attend to it, respond to it, and even accept its content as inherently true and important.

Mindfulness is a practice of becoming aware of our own mind and the thoughts and emotions that arise within it. With this awareness, we can liberate ourselves from the mind's control. Mindfulness is a practice that teaches us to look at what the mind is saying without accepting it as truth. Mindfulness creates well-being as we move away from the flight of the birds and find the space of the sky-like awareness that exists behind them. What we discover is that we can keep our attention spacious and wide and resist disappearing into each individual thought just because it has fluttered before us. Well-being at its most fundamental level is a result of separating who we are from the mind and being able to pick and choose from the stuff that the mind produces. We can choose which thoughts to engage, respond to, or ignore. Well-being is about being able to have control of our own attention and, with it, the freedom to choose our life experience, instead of allowing the mind to choose for us.

Did you ever stop to notice that everything going on in your mind—every thought, feeling, sensation, everything you are aware of—is in fact happening only in your private internal world? Your thoughts appear only to you; they're not being heard or witnessed by anyone else. As many Eastern wisdom traditions teach, there is one physical world here on earth, but billions of different internal worlds. We are all in our own separate theaters, witnessing different shows on our giant individual projection screens, and yet we behave as if we were all in the same audience watching the very same event we call life.

Why is it important to contemplate this truth? Because it is liberating to realize that what we are personally living inside our heads is not real. We are aware of our thoughts, so in that sense they are "real," and yet our thoughts do not exist outside of our awareness. There is nowhere else where the thought that is appearing to you at this moment is actually occurring. Our thoughts are not solid, like trees or rocks that exist outside of us in some tangible way. If at this moment you hear a thought about a friend—say, something specific that your friend did to you and what you want to say in response—and you don't engage that thought, it will literally cease to exist. How freeing is it to know that if we don't attend to a thought, answer it, change it, identify with it, and all the rest, it will subside? If we let a thought be nothing, then that's what it will be.

It can be a bit frightening to realize that we are the only ones living the experience we are living and that what we call our experience doesn't exist except for an instant inside our minds. So, too, it can be unsettling to consider that there really is no shared experience going on. What's more, we do not choose the thoughts and feelings that appear before us—they just appear in our awareness and then disappear, like fireflies in the night. We simply cannot know what thoughts are made of and where they come from.

If each of us is hearing a different soundtrack and watching a different movie, then to whom or what are all these individual and separate performances appearing? Who or what is the larger audience, the collective awareness within which all these individual movies occur?

PART 6

mindfulness practice
for the digital age

take a breath

n this next section, you will notice an absence of research studies, statistics, and before-and-after accounts. This absence is deliberate because this section on mindfulness is not meant to be more food for the already overfed monkey mind. I am leaving out the befores and afters to prevent mindfulness from becoming the next task you have to accomplish, the next spiritual goal you need to reach. If you walk away from this book with an intellectual understanding of mindfulness and its benefits but without a shift in the embodied experience of your actual life, then I will have failed you.

Please don't put mindfulness in a box up on the shelf as another interesting item in your storehouse of spiritual wisdom. I want to prevent the mind from co-opting mindfulness and reducing it to another identity to claim: "the mindful me." Mindfulness practice is not another opportunity to become a better and more spiritual version of your self.

Don't "do" mindfulness because you "should." It is important to protect mindfulness from becoming the new "there," which will allow you to be "here" only when you reach "there." In the same way, we also don't want mindfulness to become the new "then," which will make "now" important when "then" happens.

Mindfulness practice is more than an interesting technique that will make you feel better. It is that, but it is also a fundamentally different way of seeing the world and being inside your life. I want you to experience and live the profound difference a mindful life offers and to start doing so now, whether it looks like the "right now" or not.

If mindfulness can be safeguarded from becoming just another idea, it can offer you a genuine paradigm shift in the way you relate to life. Your relationship with this very moment will be infused with a sense of sincere curiosity and even awe.

As you read through this last section of the book, let the felt sense of the words marinate inside you, and as best you can, try not to figure out how to make that happen. Allow and welcome whatever sensations and thoughts appear, but don't build any of what arises into a new theory on life, a new self-improvement plan, or a new spiritual goal. Simply pay attention to the moment that's unfolding right now, inside and outside of you, and trust that in doing so, everything that needs to be happening is happening.

the practice of mindfulness

Mindfulness is the act of paying attention, on purpose, to this present moment and doing so without judgment. It is the practice of waking up inside our lives. Mindfulness has one destination: now. As a practice, it stops the mind's movement forward and backward and deposits us here, where we are. Mindfulness asks us to come home into ourselves to inquire, *What is happening here, at the center of this now? What's it like if I let everything be exactly as it is?* Simply put, mindfulness is the practice of treating our life like it really matters. It offers space, silence, and stillness all rolled into one.

Mindfulness practice removes the belief that we constantly have to be getting somewhere else, making life happen, and changing what is. It teaches us to get interested in, allow, and trust the present moment. It permits us to know this "now" as a place where life is always available and always happening without effort. In mindfulness practice, we come to experience the present moment and ourselves as complete, exactly as they are, lacking nothing. With mindfulness as our way of seeing, we learn to experience whatever is here, now, as whole—and in that way, as what is supposed to be right now, whether it's likable or not. Mindfulness practice removes "should be" and replaces it with "what is." It is our awakened presence that is the key to unlocking these truths.

Mindfulness is both a direct practice (something we do in meditation for a set period of time, ideally every day) and a way of living, an awareness that becomes inherent to everything we do and are.

A Morning Practice

Every morning we mindfully begin the day by bringing our attention to the senses, the breath, and the body. We start by simply paying attention to the sounds arising in our environment. We don't need to label or explain the sounds but rather just allow our ears to receive what's coming in and stay present with what's being received. This is an immediate and gentle way to enter "now," as it takes no effort to hear. What's more, wherever we are and whenever we choose to listen, sound is always present to pay attention to, no matter how subtle it may be.

After a minute or two of paying attention to the sounds that arise, we bring our attention to the breath. We tune into the breath as it enters the body, wherever we directly sense it, whether the point is at the nostrils or in the chest or in the belly. We also sense into the gap at the top of an inhalation, that space before the exhalation begins, as well as at the bottom of an exhalation, before the next inhalation commences. We ride the breath like a swinging door, pausing at each arc's end. When thoughts about the day to come or anything else interrupt the experience of sensing—which they will—we don't make a big deal of it. Instead, we just bring our attention back to the feel of the breath, noting (and celebrating) the moment of waking up to our having disappeared. Both our not-there-ness and our aware return are mindfulness in action—the practice at work.

After five to ten minutes of staying present with the breath, we turn our attention to the particular sensations happening inside the body, whatever is moving through the body at this moment. We sense, *What is it like inside my body right now?* We feel any tingling, heaviness, tightness, swirling, warmth—whatever sensations are present. The idea is not to determine whether it *should* be like this but rather to sense what it *is* like. We don't ask why the sensations are happening, and we don't judge whether the sensations are good or bad or, for that matter, what they mean. If a judgment or a story about the sensations does come, we simply observe that too.

Following this, we take a few minutes to notice the conditions of the mind, observing whether the ocean of mind is busy and choppy or quiet, with few thoughts tossing about. The purpose of noticing is not to get involved in the contents of the thoughts but, rather, simply to take note of the mind's conditions, the way a sailor looks out at the sea to take a reading. So, too, we remain aware throughout this process that everything that is witnessed will soon change and pass out of view.

Next, we notice if there are any emotions present as we begin this day. We observe whether such emotions are in the foreground—that is, very present or acute—or more in the background—dull and a bit vague, like wallpaper feelings. Again, the idea is not to dive into the stories of our emotions, not to add anything to them, not to get involved in the who, what, where, when, and whys. We simply want to experience all that our immediate "now" includes. We just allow what is here to be here, without having to do anything to make it different or better.

And, finally, we become aware of awareness itself, the presence within which all of these phenomena are occurring, sensing the space through which these ever-changing movements are passing. We point our attention toward that to which these sensations, thoughts, and feelings are appearing. And we inquire (but do not answer), *Who or what is it that is experiencing all these phenomena we call life? What's here that's not these phenomena?*

If possible it's best to begin the day with this practice, so that nothing in the busyness of life ends up getting in the way of it happening. When it's not yet habit, practice can easily slip away from us, as other things pile up and it feels impossible to sit down for even a few minutes. Depositing time into our awareness bank early in the day is the best way to make sure we practice and thus reap the benefits, before the day's distractions pull us away and convince us that there are more important items on our to-do list. When we take time out from our schedule to practice, no matter how busy we are, we find that we actually have more time to live. We are awake and present in the time we do have, and as a result, our practice actually expands our sense of time.

The practice of mindfulness is simply to notice and allow whatever is moving through our field of awareness and to dwell in our direct experience of this moment, without trying to change it, while we ask ourselves, *What is happening right now, and can I be with it?* At its core, mindfulness is about discovering the extraordinary ordinary and allowing it to unfold in our midst.

To add this simple exercise to our day trains us to become more conscious of where we actually are. For some of us, practicing this exercise may be the only time in the day when our attention is in the same location as our body, when our awareness is in sync with our physical presence. With practice, however, this compartmentalized experience of mindfulness will change. Mindfulness practice teaches us how to get interested in "now" and how to build a relationship with "now" that is curious and friendly, not fearful and defensive. It trains us to turn ourselves and this moment into a destination, a place we're interested in knowing, not just knowing *about* but directly experiencing. When we include this practice in our daily lives, we are expressing and realizing our intention to meet life as it actually is.

In addition to a daily, uninterrupted, fifteen- to thirty-minute mindfulness meditation, it's a good idea to incorporate mini practice sessions into the day, little check-ins at many times throughout the day. Every hour on the hour, for example, we can drop into our direct experience and notice what is happening right now in our field of awareness, in our bodies, minds, and surroundings (wearing a rubber band on our wrist can help us remember to check in). We're not looking for something particular, certainly not for something earth-shattering. We're just observing to see what is true right here, right now.

The practice of mindfulness requires remembering to be mindful. So we take a moment to experience a full in-breath and out-breath before we log onto Facebook, or we listen closely to the sounds arising as we ride the bus. We feel each foot meet the ground as we walk the supermarket aisles or tune into our heartbeats while we work at our desks. We experience the sensations of chewing and the precise taste of our food. Wherever we are, whatever we're doing, we can take just a few moments to pause and notice what our life is actually made of. With a simple invitation and the use of our senses as both our vehicle and our anchor, we can usher ourselves into this present moment, and in so doing, into our lives, right here, at the center of "now."

These "stop and drops," if you will, serve as short meditations that deepen the practice and strengthen the muscle of awareness. After some time, the awareness we are consciously cultivating becomes natural and habitual. Mindfulness then becomes how we behave in the world. It infuses our being. As a result of mindfulness practice, we discover that we are present and awake and really living. And what better result could there possibly be?

40

stocking your mindfulness toolbox

We are all different, so when it comes to techniques, what lights one person's world on fire might not even heat the embers for another. So notice which techniques are most powerful in bringing you into your "now" and your direct experience. Once you know what works for you, you can stock your mindfulness toolbox with those techniques. The real key in all this is practice. There is no substitute for practice, and there is no better moment than now to meet "now."

Throughout this chapter, I will pose questions, but once again, they are not riddles for the mind to untangle. They are pointers that, when pondered, will lead you to a new way of seeing and experiencing life.

Am I Here?

At its core, to be here, to be mindful, requires that we not be somewhere else. The first tool of mindfulness is learning to notice where your attention actually is. Throughout the day, simply ask yourself, *Am I here?* And then follow that question with these: *Who is it that asks this question? And who responds?* Don't give these questions to the mind. Just invite them into the body. Practice this simple but profound inquiry until it becomes habit.

Am I Breathing?

Unlike the mind, the physical body is always in the present moment. The body cannot and does not seek to be anywhere but here. It doesn't even *seek* here so much as it simply *is* here. As such, we can make use of the body's always-present nature as a vehicle to help us come back to this moment. By dropping into the body and experiencing it directly, we hitch a ride straight into "now."

There is a wonderful expression: "God is as close as your next breath." We are always just a breath away from presence, and we can always come home via our next breath, simply by bringing our attention to it and experiencing it directly. Feel the sensation of the breath moving through you. Ask yourself, *Who is doing the breathing, and who is being breathed?* Become intimate with the experience and miracle of the breath, which is always available, always here—life itself.

Staying Present with Sound

Tune into the sounds that are arising right now in your environment, near and far, subtle and vibrant. Allow your ears to simply receive whatever sounds arise, without having to filter them through the mind or assign any meaning to what is received. Simply be ears hearing, with no story attached. Ask yourself, *Who hears these sounds?*

The Sensation of Sensation

Feel the sensations that are occurring inside the body right now. Don't describe them to yourself with words, judge whether you like them, or comment on what they mean. Rather than noticing that your feet are tingling, feel the tingling directly. Rather than thinking about the ache in your back, feel the achiness itself. Drop the separate "you" who is doing the experiencing, the narrator, and instead experience the sensations directly, not from the mind but from inside the body itself. Now ask yourself, *Who or what experiences these sensations?*

Inside and Outside

Bring your attention to what is being seen right now, the images that your eyes are perceiving. While maintaining mindful awareness of the seen, add what is being heard, the sounds entering your ears. Hold both the seen and the heard simultaneously. Now, notice what is happening inside the body, the physical sensations arising. Hold the awareness of all three at once: sight, sound, and body. Ask yourself, *What is it that can be aware of both the inside and the outside?*

Awareness of Mind

Bring your attention to what your mind is saying to you right now. Listen in on the thoughts, words, ideas, beliefs, preferences—the whole circus that is parading through your mind. Become aware, too, of the feeling states arising in you. Don't judge, respond, or comment on the contents of what you are noticing. Just observe the thoughts and feelings present, now. Take a seat in the audience of your own show. Notice also what's there in the space between thoughts, in the gap, before a new thought has formed. Look to see what else is there, behind the thoughts, beyond the feelings. Ask yourself, *Who is the mind talking to? Who or what is listening?*

Widening Your View with the Three *S*'s

When they're directly experienced, silence, stillness, and spaciousness—the Three *S*'s—are the gateways to knowing yourself as pure presence, pure awareness. They are the portals to your infinite nature.

Silence. Listen for the silence that is always here under the noise of mind. Tune into the sense and the sound of inner silence. Shift your attention from the objects of mind noise to the silence within which the objects of noise appear.

Stillness. Feel the stillness that is here, in the background, behind and under all that is moving through consciousness. Sense the unmoving presence, the feeling of just being, which remains steady while our personal weather systems pass through. Experience that deep, steady stillness, which doesn't move and isn't disturbed by that which is moving through it.

Spaciousness. Open your view so it becomes wide, panoramic. Become aware of the infinite spaciousness within which thoughts, feelings, and sensations appear. Sense it. Sense the open sky that is behind, in front of, under, over, and in between the phenomena that travel through. Transfer your attention from the objects that are manifesting in consciousness to the vastness that contains them, from the ever-changing scenery to the unchanging space within which it arises. Realign your attention from the momentary to the timeless. Inquire within, *What is here behind all this that dances in consciousness? What is the screen upon which this show becomes visible?*

Feeling Presence

Close your eyes and feel the sensation of your own presence, the felt sense of just being. Ask within, *Am I alive right now? Am I conscious?* Notice where you go in your body to feel for the answers. Don't think; just experience your own alive presence. Tune into the body's particular sense of existing, the physically experienced hum that allows you to know you are. Drop into that particular sensation that is "I am"—not "I am X" or "I am Y" but, simply, "I am."

From "What's Next?" to "What's Here?"

For a moment, imagine there is no next event, next task, next person, or next anything to get to. Remove all "nexts." Invite yourself to stop preparing, planning, or getting ready for something else. Deliberately delete all the "what elses." Meet "now" with "nowhere and nothing left to get to." Ask yourself, *What is here, now?* Invite yourself to feel the center of now. Sense the freedom and aliveness in no future and no past, in just this.

The End and the Beginning

Imagine that these are the last few minutes of your life in this body, as this "you." There is nothing left to prepare for, organize, or accomplish.

There is only this "now" and nothing after it. Drop into right now and that fundamental sense of "youness" that has always been here, from the time you were a "you." Feel that unchanging essence of who you are, which has remained while all else—thoughts, feelings, situations, body, beliefs, relationships, et cetera—have been on a course of constant change. Feel the "you" that is timeless, that witnesses time, that is the very core of your being. Ask yourself, *What is this that has always been here while all else has come and gone in front of it?*

⏻

Each of these practices holds the power to boomerang us back into this present moment. They are not concepts but practices to be practiced. Even a few moments of consistent practice can change our experience and our lives. If we are not here, not present, then quite literally we are not here, not in our lives. We are missing in action, lost in the ether, disappeared into our devices, distractions, and the stories that exist only in our own minds.

Ironically, we in the virtual world are consumed with FoMO, the Fear of Missing Out. We check our screens again and again for the great thing that we don't want to miss out on. And yet, as a result, many of us miss out on the most important thing of all, life. We ought to worry less about missing out on the next tweet and focus more on our own existence. Every moment from which we are absent is a profound loss, particularly when you consider how brief our stay here is. Stock your mindfulness toolbox, and practice, practice, and then practice some more. The benefit of such practice is nothing short of life itself.

41

mindfulness for the uncooperative mind

When we learn about mindfulness, regardless of how wonderful the benefits sound, many of us feel a strong resistance to actually sitting still and meditating, that is, the formal practice of mindfulness. The mind loves to learn about new practices but is not so keen on actually practicing them, particularly when they involve doing "nothing" while witnessing the behavior of the mind itself. People often tell me they are going to start thinking about meditating, consider getting started on it, or, better yet, study it. This usually means that the time for action is still some ways away, because thinking about meditating is kind of the opposite of meditating.

We are often not ready to dive into a practice that will most certainly create change, no matter how much we say and believe we want change. More often than not, the resistance manifests as some reason why mindfulness doesn't apply to our particular personality, life, or psychological story—essentially, why it's great for everyone else and has stuck around for centuries but just isn't quite right for "this me." And yet, when examined more closely, most of the obstacles that we believe stand in the way of living mindfully are not obstacles at all. In fact, with the light of mindfulness upon them, our fears and resistances become new sensations to notice. Let's look at some of these fears and misconceptions.

The Big Nonobstacles; or, Misconceptions on Mindfulness and Meditation

1 "Mindfulness does not work in a modern, scheduled life."

As one client put it, "I have kids, which means that I am constantly planning for the future—camps, holidays, dinner recipes, weekend babysitting, et cetera. I can't just be here in the now. It's not practical for a real life. Maybe if you're a nomad wandering in India, but mindfulness is of no use to a working mom in New York City!"

Many of my clients share the belief that having to do anything that involves or is about the future, such as making plans, disqualifies them from being mindful. In truth, mindfulness simply means being conscious, or aware, of what is happening inside and outside of you right now. It's being awake to life as it is unfolding. Planning for the future and attending to the past are necessities in modern life, but while the contents of what we are planning are related to the future, the planning itself is something that is happening right now. Perhaps we are making an airplane reservation: the airplane will take off in the future, but conversing with the agent, experiencing physical sensations in the hand holding the phone, receiving thoughts and feelings about what you're hearing, taking in sounds from the room, feeling emotions about the upcoming travel—all of these and a thousand other events are occurring right now. Making plans mindfully simply means paying attention to the experience of making plans, being awake to what it is like for you to live this moment of planning.

The subject of the moment is irrelevant because the moment itself is always happening right here and right now. Nothing can ever be happening in any time but now. If at this moment your body is breathing, then there is a present experience available to you, and thus mindfulness is possible in your modern, scheduled life.

2 "Mindfulness means focusing on my breath or meditating constantly, which isn't practical in everyday life. Mindfulness takes you out of real life."

A client put this objection this way: "When a strong emotion comes up, like when I get really angry at my boss at work, I can't always check out of the conversation and start listening to my breath or chant, 'Om.' Mindfulness is not viable in real-life, tough situations."

Practicing mindfulness does not require checking out of life; in fact, just the opposite is true—it requires checking in to life. When a strong feeling such as anger arises, practicing mindfulness means paying attention to what that anger feels like in the body, how it manifests, what thoughts and stories accompany it—everything that is happening inside and outside you as you experience the anger right now. Practicing mindfulness means witnessing that strong emotion with full presence, watching the weather of anger erupt in the sky of awareness. Sometimes it does help to come back to the breath, just for a moment, to get grounded in your body and not spin off in the storm of the mind—but this is not necessary for practicing mindfulness. Mindfulness means staying here, where you are, with whatever is arising in the present moment, and meeting your direct experience, your life, as it actually is.

3 "I can't be mindful with this mind, my mind as it is. When my mind is different, calmer perhaps, then, possibly, mindfulness can happen."

Many people believe that mindfulness requires a certain kind of mind, a baseline of peacefulness or tranquility, and that their minds, as they are, are far too wild to practice such a skill. In fact, mindfulness does not depend on any particular kind of mind and certainly not a calm one. If mindfulness required a calm mind, it would have died out as a practice a long time ago. In the same way that meditation is an investigation of your inner world as it is, right now, without preference or judgment, mindfulness is just an honest look at the way your mind, your direct experience, and your life are at any given moment. You are not more mindful if you discover that you like the moment you are living and less mindful if what you become aware of is not pleasing. Mindfulness only means that you are noticing, becoming conscious of, and dwelling in your direct experience, instead of pushing it away—and if you are trying to push it away, you notice that, too.

Mindfulness is not about the content of what you find when you drop down into yourself. It's about dropping down into yourself with an attitude of compassionate curiosity. If what you notice when you turn the spotlight on yourself is that your mind is wild and desperate for one of your devices and a way out of here, then mindfulness would entail bringing an open and kind curiosity to that tech-craving impulse. And so it goes. There are no right answers in mindfulness, no better things to discover under the lens of your own attention, and no better kind of mind to practice with. We practice mindfulness to see and allow what is. The only requirements for mindfulness are a mind to practice with, a willingness to try to stay present (whether we like what we find or not), and an interest in meeting yourself and your actual experience in this precise moment.

4 **"Others can risk dropping into 'now,' but not me. If I pay attention to the present moment, I am going to discover things that I don't want to see and can't deal with. Once that happens, I'll end up getting stuck in those things, and I'll never be able to get free. For me, it's better to just stay away from 'now.'"**

For someone with this particular misconception, there is no more important practice than mindfulness. Mindfulness teaches us how to be the masters of our own attention. It's about learning how to simply witness what is moving through our awareness—the thoughts, feelings, and sensations that are vying for our notice—but without having to award them the attention they demand. In this way, it is a practice of breaking habits—namely, the habit of having to engage with whatever thought appears before us simply because it has appeared.

Mindfulness is about learning to watch but not engage, which is something we never knew we were allowed to or even could do!

There are different kinds of thoughts. Some are easy to notice and let pass, while others are quite sticky, carrying trauma, loss, or some other gripping story attached to them. As such, they seem to have the power to entice us down the rabbit hole. Before we know what's happened, we've fallen in and are lost in stories. And yet this is just what mindfulness training is designed to address: we learn to hold our seat at the center of our experience as the thought storms swirl around us, and we refrain from diving into their contents. Only through practice do we learn to remain still when strong energies are occurring, simply witnessing their presence and the sensations that accompany them.

In mindfulness training, we develop the extraordinary strength and confidence that comes from knowing we can stay present and still even in a tsunami of thoughts and feelings, without being swallowed up by them. We come to trust that we can be safe anywhere, knowing that the contents of our "now," the mind's rants, do not determine our equanimity. Rather, it is our steady and fierce awareness that determines whether we are fundamentally okay. So, too, we discover the great wisdom that comes from knowing that the most difficult and intense of thoughts pass, like all phenomena. We realize that all thoughts gain strength from only one thing: our attention.

In addition, there is a belief with this particular misconception about mindfulness that our fearful thoughts are always lurking nearby, waiting for us in the shadows of the present moment. But more often than not, what people find is that when they do turn their attention to the now, the fearful and feared thoughts are not here. Oddly, many of us then go looking for such thoughts, wondering why they're not appearing in awareness, but they often come back empty-handed. It is often the case that the thoughts and beliefs we have created about what we will discover in the now prove to be more frightening than anything we actually discover. Through mindfulness training, we come to see that the thoughts about the thoughts are products of the same mind, whose show we learn to witness without falling under its spell.

Mindfulness is the practice we need most when we fear the now. Mindfulness gives us the direct experience—not just a conceptual understanding—that as awareness, we are infinitely larger than any thought or feeling our minds can throw at us. As a result, no matter what might appear here now, we do not need to fear the present moment, not when we contain the strength of awareness.

5 **"If I am meditating correctly, my mind will be calm and empty. If I still have thoughts while meditating, if my mind doesn't calm down, it means that my mindfulness practice is a failure, and that I'm a failure. With enough meditation practice, I should be able to stop thinking altogether."**

The real purpose of mindfulness meditation is not to calm the mind or ourselves, although it may be a reason we begin the practice. Rest assured that you have not failed if your mind does not become like a still pool as a result of meditating regularly, and most certainly you have not failed because your mind continues to generate thoughts. The purpose of mindfulness meditation is to change the place from which we are looking at our thoughts—that is, to build an awareness in which we can observe the nature of our mind, its natural chaos, which these days includes the added chaos of our tech infusion.

It is the nature of the mind, and even more so of a mind that has been plugged into technology, to spew out material randomly and relentlessly, whether meditating or not. Some people who have practiced for decades continue to experience an uninterrupted stream of thoughts and images, both on and off the meditation cushion. The purpose of meditation is not to change the basic nature of the mind, not to turn it into something it isn't. While we may hope that it changes and calms down when we no longer engage with its theories and complaints, the real purpose of meditation is to observe the mind as it is.

In the digital age, observing the mind often means observing a frantic, ravenous, and insatiable animal, jacked up and saturated with entertainment, communication, information, and just plain stuff—a mind that can't stop moving and wanting more and more stuff. In meditation, the mind's moving and wanting can be seen from a place that is not frantic. With practice, we can witness the mind's condition on technology and off technology.

Meditation allows us not only to observe but also to shift our allegiance and identification. We become less identified with the chaotic mind itself, the ticker tape that runs through our heads, the roller coaster of wanting our minds ride. We become more steadily aligned with the awareness that witnesses and the spaciousness in which the mind's dramas play out. The purpose of mindfulness meditation is really just to become more skilled and comfortable with the process of looking and to become more rooted in the place that is looking—rather than being tossed about by what is being looked at. In meditation we hone our ability to see clearly, without holding an idea of what we should be seeing.

⏻

So why all this talk about mindfulness meditation when it's possible that nothing about the mind's behavior changes as a result of it? Surely we can create an app that would be far easier, more immediate, and as effective at silencing the mind and providing welcome relief. Why do something every day when at the end of it all we might have to deal with the same crazy monkey living inside our heads?

It is counterintuitive, really: we set out with the clear instruction not to change what we find, and yet, as a result, everything changes once it is seen and offered permission to be as it is. What happens as a result of witnessing our own minds without judgment or commentary is that over time we realize we are *not* those minds, not the thoughts, beliefs, ideas, and all else that they create. The mind fires off without our help because it is designed to generate content. But the whole show happens with or without our participation, without the need for a thinker. The purpose of meditation is not to change our minds but to awaken the aspect of self that is aware of the mind.

Meditation is nothing fancy but everything necessary, particularly now, when we so desperately need a place just to be and a sense of our own selves that is not under the influence of digital mania. The next time you have the thought that mindfulness doesn't apply to you because of the way your life is, your mind is, your circumstances are, or who you are, notice that thought and pay attention to what it feels like in your body to have that thought. Allow the thought to be there, without judging it, and take note of what other thoughts accompany it, if any. Ask yourself, *Who is listening to this thought? Who, if anyone, is believing it?* Before you know it, the you who doesn't live in India and can't practice mindfulness or meditate properly, for that matter, will be practicing mindfulness after all.

being in the moment
when we don't like the moment

always chuckle when I see the kind of photograph that typically accompanies anything written about mindfulness. Nine times out of ten, the photo is shot from behind a person (usually a young, thin woman) who is sitting cross-legged on the beach, looking out at the water, as the sun sets or rises on the horizon. The implication is that this peaceful, beautiful scene is what presence feels like. The truth is that if life were a beach at sunset, we wouldn't have to work so hard at being present in it.

If what we were hearing was the lapping of waves against the sand, we would want to listen to the sound of now. But what happens when what we're hearing is the sound of someone's iPhone ringing every fifteen seconds and we're being told that our plane still hasn't been cleared for takeoff? If what we smell is the fresh, salty air coming off the sea, we might well want to breathe in what is here. But what happens when we're smelling the cleaning solution the gym attendant is spraying? If what we're feeling is the warm sand against our toes, we'll probably want to sink into the present sensation. But what happens when what we're feeling is the cold slush soaking into our pants as the bus wheels spray us? If what we're seeing is the pinks and blues of a glorious sunset, we might well want to keep our eyes open to what is now. But what happens when what we're looking at is a homeless person hunkered down for the night under filthy blankets on an icy sidewalk? How do we live in the present moment, mindful of what we are directly experiencing, when the present moment is painful or unpleasant?

Life includes experiences that we like and want as well as those that we don't like and don't want. We are certainly better at being present in the moments we like, but we need more practice staying in the ones we don't. Many people ask me why it's important to try to be present in the bad moments and why we shouldn't try to get out of them quickly or figure out how not to be in them at all. As one friend put it, "It seems like it would be wiser to focus on how I'm going to get another drink rather than how I'm going to wake up in a situation that causes pain." Our assumption is that being present in what we call the bad moments is somehow agreeing to them, surrendering to them, and giving up all efforts to change them. We believe that in order to keep things good in our lives, we must brace against, ignore, or reject anything that is not good. This is an incorrect assumption with profound consequences.

Agreeing to be mindful in the hard moments is simply acknowledging that what is happening is happening and that we are in it. We accept that this is what we are living right now, whether or not we like it. Some people find it is easier to work with the word *allow* as opposed to *accept*. We allow what is to be, just for a moment, and we stop wishing it away or trying to make it something else. Inside ourselves, we say, *Yes, this is so*, and, if appropriate, *Yes, this is also painful*. This yes, this acceptance, this allowing to be, is fundamentally different from *Yes, I want this* or *Yes, I like this*. When we allow the moment to include what it includes, we give up fighting against it. We relinquish the idea that what is happening should not be happening, and certainly not happening to us. We stop pretending the moment is otherwise. Being in the truth of what is, without fighting it, we give ourselves the gift of our own real company. We sit down with ourselves, lovingly, as we would with a child after they've lived through a hard day. We are in the moment *with* ourselves, exactly the way life is right now, and at last we are not alone.

Our own compassionate company is a form of loving-kindness, and it brings profound relief to our pain. We finally have our own kindness, our attention and presence, accompanying us in what we are actually living. When we give ourselves permission to be with ourselves in the moments that don't feel good—the moments that may even feel like hell—ironically, we experience a warmth and a wholeness. We come home to the truth and to ourselves. Even those moments that we think will kill us don't in fact do us in. Rather, we discover that by awakening our own loving presence and our willingness to be with ourselves in the truth, the difficult moments actually make us stronger, more self-loving, and more able to be okay with life as it is. We discover that we can indeed be *in* anything.

As long as we are checking out of the moments we don't like, diving into distraction or numbing out with technology, we remain a step away from being able to change such moments. It is counterintuitive, but until we fully allow the truth of our experience, we cannot move on. We reject what is, and as a result, what is gets stuck. When we settle into and allow the truth of what is as our starting place, we plant our feet in the ground from which we can launch change. And when we are present and awake in the hard moments, we are released from the primary cause of suffering, which is fighting against reality, refusing to be where we are, and rejecting our actual lives.

It is also important to remember that when we bring mindfulness into the more challenging moments of life, we do not forfeit the awareness of how we feel or our desire for change. We don't suddenly become unconscious. We may still not want it to be the way it is, but that not wanting is included in the truth of what is. Our dislike of the moment is part of, not a contradiction to, our presence. The ability to be in the moments we don't want is a challenge that requires different skills from those we bring to being in the moments we want. Experiencing what is as it is, along with our dislike for it, enables us to form a base of compassion for ourselves. We are living in this hard moment, it is painful, we want it to be otherwise, and it is what is right now—until it isn't. All are true, and all at once. The self-compassion that arises from this process is always healing and always carries the feeling of a loving embrace.

Life presents all of us with the opportunity to be present to life off the beach—when our five-year-old child is on the floor wailing in a giant puddle of pancake syrup, when the dog needs to pee and we have a work assignment due yesterday, when we are arguing with our partner, when our health or finances are challenged, when we're sitting with a dying parent, when we're saying good-bye to a loved one. For mindfulness to take hold firmly, it belongs in every part of life, not just the parts we want to experience. The good news is that life gives us endless chances to practice being mindful in what is when what is isn't what we want. To be able to be in the moment no matter what it presents is to experience the full depth and scope of our human existence, to know ourselves in all forms and incarnations. To embrace what is happening, how we feel about it, how we wish it weren't so, how we are going to try to change it, and everything else, all at once, without denying any of it, is what it means to be fully alive. Even when we are not at the beach, we are here, tasting life—and that, in and of itself, is the real gift.

43

going all the way

The practice of mindfulness is like unpacking nested Russian dolls: we're continually discovering thoughts behind thoughts behind still more thoughts. The longer we practice, the more layers of thought and emotion we will uncover. Ultimately, mindfulness practice increases our capacity to witness what is happening inside and outside ourselves, until there is no more self to do the witnessing.

The difficulty or limitation we often run into with mindfulness practice is that we put the brakes on too soon, stop observing, and align with the thoughts our minds are presenting. We assume we've uncovered the last doll and stop unpacking. We witness an aspect of our minds, a series of thoughts, and then we get caught in the next layer of thoughts, the thoughts about the thoughts we just witnessed. What's different about this next layer of thoughts is that we believe them and fail to see them as also something separate happening in front of awareness. Our "I" gets collapsed into these thoughts, and then there is no longer an "I" there to witness them.

Here are two cases in point. A woman practicing mindfulness notices that as she walks down the street, her mind continually announces its preferences and judgments about what she is seeing. Her mind says to her: *Wow, I hate that haircut. Damn, that's a big ass. I wish I had that handbag. Geez, why are those two together?* And on it goes, without end. This woman has a normal mind. She is not particularly interested in the comments and judgments that come—in fact, she finds them quite dull—but that fact doesn't keep them from coming.

Through her mindfulness practice, this woman becomes aware that her mind ceaselessly judges everything it encounters. In other words, she has a regular human mind. Step one of her mindfulness practice is complete: she has become aware of a tendency in her mind. But then, as a result of this newfound awareness, she hears new thoughts as the mind busies itself generating new material. The new thoughts tell her that she will never be a spiritual person, that she is judgmental by nature, and that she is hopeless and awful. At this stage, she and her thoughts have become united. She believes them. What she hasn't yet done is uncovered the next Russian doll; she hasn't noticed that these judgments of herself are just another set of thoughts the mind is presenting. She falls prey to these self-critical thoughts and ceases to witness her mind generating them.

This is a classic example of what many people do in their mindfulness practice: initially, they use it to become more aware, more self-caring, and freer, but eventually they come up against something they can use against themselves. The witness, as the mind intends, believes these new judgmental thoughts, without recognizing them to be simply the mind's next layer of thoughts. At this point, the mindful witness joins with the mind's thoughts, and the practice of mindfulness is suspended until further notice.

In another example, a man attending a business meeting notices that his mind becomes very agitated and busy when a female colleague starts telling a personal story to the group. The thoughts he hears are blaming and the feeling arising is anger, because this woman is taking up everyone's time with her "nonsense." Through mindfulness practice, the man sees these thoughts and feelings and is able to refrain from trying to change, prove, or engage with them. He is aware of having the thoughts, without the inner turbulence that has accompanied such thoughts in the past. But then his mind gets sneaky and tells him that he is an angry person, just like his father, and that he will never have a partner if he feels this way when women tell their stories. He believes these new thoughts and does not see them as yet another layer of thought stuff that the mind is generating. Because he cannot see these thoughts as yet another layer of mind, the man becomes both afraid of and identified with his thoughts. At this point, he is once more a hostage of the mind, and his mindfulness practice is derailed.

Behind every thought is another thought. As we go further into our mindfulness practice, we get more skilled at seeing the line of thoughts behind the first thought, without joining our selves to any of them. We have to keep our witness goggles firmly in place as the mind morphs into subtler manifestations of itself and gets more difficult to keep track of. The mind is a master chameleon, becoming whatever it needs to become in order to keep us from seeing it as separate from who we really are. Mindfulness practice is a means to see even that chameleon-like quality.

Mindfulness is often practiced without its two core elements: curiosity and kindness. Without curiosity and kindness, our investigation of the mind becomes another exercise for the mind itself. When we notice something about the nature of our minds during mindfulness practice, whether or not we like what we see, we need to take the attitude of *Huh! Look at that. That's what my mind does. How curious!* And behind that *Huh!* are the feelings of compassion and kindness. It's like watching our child do something we know is not in their best interest, and yet, regardless of what we witness, we love our child and feel empathy for their not-yet-knowing mind as well as compassion for the suffering they will likely experience for not knowing a better way.

Mindfulness practice is not conditional: we are not observing our minds in order to make a case against it or against ourselves. When we practice, the eyes with which we look at our minds must be compassionate, or at least neutral. We must understand that this wild monkey called the human mind is after one thing—survival—and survival means being in charge. Mindfulness practice helps us realize that although we do not choose the thoughts our minds generate, we can choose whether or not we will believe them. In truth, we are the ones the mind is talking to, the ones whose attention the mind is trying desperately to keep. But the mind doesn't want us to know this.

When you reach a thought or a feeling you believe is the last one, don't stop there. Notice that you have stopped observing, that you believe yourself to be at the end of the inquiry. Watch the observer as it stops observing and starts to join itself to what it is observing. Witness identification as it happens. Ask yourself, *Who or what is perceiving that last thought or last feeling, the one that feels like the truth of who I am?* Be fierce in your observation. Keep watching everything that arises. As long as there's still a *you* watching, there's still further to go.

44

permission to be nobody

f we were to put a word in a time capsule that would represent our culture at this moment—how we live and what is important to us—that word might well be *selfie*. Many of us spend a good portion of our waking time taking pictures of ourselves and posting them on the public stage that is the Internet, hoping the world will notice and comment on our images—and possibly, hopefully, even notice the somebody behind the images. In the digital age, what we seem to care about most is becoming a somebody. While the selfie didn't birth our vast capacity for self-involvement, it did find a warm breeding ground inside us, where the phenomenon of needing to be seen as somebody already existed.

One of the most remarkable discoveries I encountered in spiritual practice is that when you go looking for this somebody, this "I" or self we consider ourselves to be and whom we are so committed to promoting, this somebody doesn't actually exist. The things by which we define ourselves are continually changing, and our "I" in fact has no fixed location.

See if you can locate or pin down what you call your "I," the solid entity that is you. Is it your body? But you are aware of your body and can witness its sensations, which means that there must be an "I" plus a body. Is "I" your mind? But you can watch your mind, too, from another level of awareness, so there must be an "I" and a mind as well. In truth, the "I" cannot be found. "I" is an idea that has an array of adjectives, memories, and stories attached to it, but "I" as an entity unto itself doesn't exist. While there is no "I" to be found, the story of "I" takes up a lot of attention, time, and energy, for it must continually be established and reestablished, assembled and reassembled, culled from memory, shored up, fed, and held together steadily and willfully.

Thankfully, meditation and other forms of spiritual inquiry allow us to see that everything we consider to be "I" is actually nothing more than a bundle of thoughts, descriptions, and beliefs about who we are, all changing and passing through awareness, like birds flying through the sky. The idea that there is a fixed "I," a somebody located somewhere, is yet another thought.

One of the most powerful spiritual teachings I ever received was actually more of an invitation than a formal teaching. My teacher, Sri Mooji, invited me to be "nobody." For the first time in my life, I was given permission to drop the story of me. I could stop expending the energy and effort it takes to keep constructing and defending the somebody living my life. When I first discovered that I could drop the whole exhausting burden that it was to be somebody, the solid identity that had to be maintained for myself and others, the somebody that *my* life was happening *to*, I felt like I had dropped a thousand-pound weight. I could leave my story of me on the side of the road and just experience life, without something else there experiencing it for me. It felt like I had finally been given permission to stop making an effort at life and instead just be. I sobbed with joy, liberated from the shackles of having to be somebody. At last, I was free to be nobody.

But being "nobody"—or, worse, "a nobody"—is not a popular pursuit in our culture—certainly not something parents encourage their kids to become. To be nobody in this culture is a fall from grace for the somebody we are supposed to be. Nobody is not really nobody, but rather a failed somebody.

From a very early age, we are conditioned to see life as something that we use to become better somebodies, better versions of ourselves, more visible, more important, and more special than the other somebodies. And if we are not working to become a better somebody, then we believe we are not fully living or doing our jobs as productive human beings.

We are not only conditioned to believe that we need the story of a "me" in order to live a productive life but also that the story is needed for life to continue at all. We fear no separate "I" as if it were death.

Without an "I" to experience life, there can be no experience. But what we were taught is often not what is best for our overall well-being.

Try this as an adventure—the adventure of getting to be nobody. The only instruction on this adventure is that you stop trying to be a better somebody, stop trying to be a somebody at all. Rest assured that you can always go back to being a somebody. Somebody will be there waiting, I promise. Just for a day, though, drop the story of your "I" and the whole bundle of thoughts about who you are, what your life is about, and all that you intend to be. The next time you are compelled to tweet out your somebodyhood, pause and try on being nobody instead. Observe who and what is there when there is no story of "I" to buoy and protect. Notice the energy and spontaneity that is freed up when your "I" doesn't need to be continually rolled out into a particular shape for everyone to see and then fortified and defended as *that*. As you try this exercise, however, be careful not to become a new "I-less I." Don't allow "nobody" to become the next identity you need to uphold.

In truth, what you may find is that without the story of "I," life does continue, but who we are is liberated from the effort, constraints, and separation that a solid identity imposes. Without the story of "I," with nothing to defend and no somebody to uphold, we are free simply to live, now, without the baggage and strategies that maintaining the story of "I" demands. Thoughts and feelings pass through us, but they don't stick to an "I" or determine anything about our identities.

When we let go of having to be a somebody, an amazing thing happens: life actually starts happening, not *to* us, but just happening, on its own. This moment unfolds, and we are inside it, fluid and porous, unfolding with it and as it, no longer trying to hold onto a fixed and solid "I" in the midst of the ever-changing flow. Dropping the idea of a somebody who is the one living our lives and thus is separated from life is like taking off a thick overcoat that has been muffling us from our experience, blocking us from feeling truly alive. We do not need an "I" to live our lives for us. We already *are* life. With permission to be nobody, we get to experience nothing less than a true rebirth. Without an "I," we are reborn as life itself.

Enjoy nobody's journey. Savor the paradox that the less "I" is there to enjoy it, the more joyful and alive the journey will be.

epilogue

freedom *in*, not *from*

In thinking about the conclusion for this book, I found myself a bit perplexed. I cover many topics in this work, all of which have something to do with technology—how it is changing who we are, how we experience ourselves, and the ways we behave and interact. So what do I say now, at the end of all this? As I pondered this question, one phrase kept returning, a phrase I originally heard Jeff Foster, a spiritual teacher, share. It's a phrase that has forever changed the way I relate to challenge and difficulty: "Freedom *in*, not freedom *from*."

Technology is not going anywhere. I think that is a fair assumption. In fact, it might even be fair to predict that human beings will go somewhere else before technology does. But no matter what the future holds, getting free from technology is no longer a real option if we are living in the world and not a cave in a forest. If we want to play in the game of life as it is now, we have to find ways to create a healthy relationship with technology, to form a handshake between our human needs and our technological opportunities. We need to find freedom *in* technology, not *from* technology. This is not only possible but also closer than we think.

Freedom, in this case, is born out of awareness. Freedom *in* technology means awakening to the fact that we can mindfully choose for ourselves how we want to interact with technology, as well as how we want to be in relationship with ourselves as we live with and through technology. Freedom involves breaking out of the unconsciousness that technology induces, the assumption that the way we are using technology and what it does to us is out of our control—rather than something we are actually deciding on a moment-to-moment basis. Freedom *in* means awakening to the truth of what is happening in our outer and inner worlds and then mindfully addressing what is happening, with our deeper wisdom as our guide.

While everything we know is changing, what remains unchanging is what we as humans need in order to be nourished emotionally and spiritually, to feel grounded and connected to ourselves and other people, and to experience meaning. Freedom *in* means making use of technology but staying fiercely mindful and protective of that which is most important—what we need more than anything else to be well, calm, and centered, and to lead lives of substance. We need to generate and honor the choices that allow us to create the kind of lives we ultimately want, even when those choices differ from what everyone else is doing. Freedom *in* technology is about taking back the steering wheel of our own lives and refusing to become technology's passenger, careening about aimlessly as we chase its blinking lights.

Although we behave as if we are enslaved by technology, as if we have no say in the matter, in fact we are not slaves, and we need not despair. We have simply lost the awareness of our own rights and, with that, of our own power, autonomy, and wisdom. The cage door is open—we just think we're locked inside. We need to remember that we can choose freedom, starting now.

In truth, we know what we need in order to feel well. We must remember to consult and trust that knowing, our intuition and life experience, and stop ceding what we know to a source that is not taking good care of our human longings. Awake, present, and conscious, with our own deepest well-being as the gauge for our choices, we can make use of technology without surrendering even a drop of our freedom.

When you are having a meal with your child, partner, or a friend, you have the choice to turn off your phone if being truly present together is what you genuinely crave. When, on the other hand, you need a plane reservation and must navigate a complicated site to make that happen, you can bring your compassionate and mindful attention to your experience of technology, acknowledging the truth of what it is like to be a human living in the digital age. Making a conscious choice in service to your deeper needs, as well as acknowledging your experience when your choices are limited, are both forms of self-compassion, and both generate well-being.

Human beings are a most remarkable species. Despite the rumors to the contrary, we are far more intelligent and contain infinitely more potential than technology could ever possess. There is no way to copy and paste the human heart or the human spirit, and there is no way to download the wisdom a human being possesses. We need to remember this truth and bow to our highest selves, which know what we need in order to live a good life. *We need to remember to remember the most important thing.*

Einstein said, "There are two ways to live: you can live as if nothing is a miracle, or you can live as if everything is a miracle."[1] It's time to remember that we human beings are the real miracle, not our devices. Our human-being-ness—remembered, respected, and protected, above all other pleasures and pursuits—is our freedom.

The not so good news is that we have been building bad habits and living with technology without awareness—asleep at the wheel of our lives. The good, even great, news is that going forward, the choice about how we will be in relationship with technology, the world around us, and ourselves is up to us.

acknowledgments

Every book, I believe, contains a blending of influences from everyone we have ever known. But there isn't time or space to thank all those whom I carry in my heart and who are part of the "me" who wrote this book. So for now I will keep the list short.

To my agent, Priya Doraswamy, you are steadfast, reliable, and eternally optimistic. Together we rode through some extreme peaks and valleys on this project, and through it all, you stayed committed, encouraging, and helpful. Most importantly, you are not just my agent, you are also my friend. To my editor, Vesela Simic, thank you for providing a profoundly corrective editorial experience. You are generous of spirit, wise, efficient, and heart rich. Working with you is a delight! To Haven Iverson, Leslie Brown, Tami Simon, and the entire Sounds True team: thank you for your awareness and insight; I am so happy that my book had the opportunity to grow in the beautiful garden you create.

To Jan Bronson: thank you always for your presence, kindness, and for accompanying me through life. To my sisters in heart, Bronwen Knappenberger, Shauna Storey Grissett, Melissa McCool, and Karen Greenberg: thank you for your support and love, which I feel wherever I am. To my mom, Diane Shainberg, thank you, forever, for your unconditional love and wisdom. To Frederic, thank you for suggesting that I create this book and for your willingness to be helpful in countless ways. And mostly for loving our girls the way that you do. To Juliet and Gretchen, you are my daughters, my ground, my joy, and the light that illuminates my heart. While mindfulness may not mean much to you now, my wish is for you to experience the presence and freedom that these practices can offer. May you be empowered to choose for yourselves how you want to live in this virtual world. May you feel the divine mystery of life and stay connected to your deepest wisdom, no matter what distractions vie for your attention. Remember, it is safe to turn your attention away from the bright lights and screens that beckon and come home to yourselves.

And to my teachers, Sri Mooji, Tara Brach, Miranda Macpherson, Jonathan Foust, Grace Bubeck, Loch Kelly, and Stephan Bodian, thank you for pointing me, in your different ways, toward knowing and trusting infinite grace.

appendix

a 30-day tech detox

A 30-Day Tech Detox was not originally a part of my vision for this book. But then a woman I know and respect, someone I consider wise and aware and thus immune to tech addiction, literally begged me to create a detox program for her and everyone else she knows. She wasn't using technology only for work, which she needs to do, but was craving it all the time. She didn't know how to stop it from taking over her personal life. Even with all her wisdom, my friend confessed that she was addicted to her smartphone and had taken to locking it in her car and parking a long distance from her house so that she wouldn't be able to access it at home. This was the only strategy she could come up with to cut down on her use and regain control of her life. The fact that she had to resort to this desperate method, which left her thinking about her phone all night, scared her. She knew this wasn't an acceptable solution to her problem. It wasn't even foolproof, because she still had the keys to her car, and, more importantly, it didn't solve the larger problem of her dependence. Although highly aware of her addiction, my friend felt powerless.

The same week as I had that conversation, I ran into a friend from the gym. He told me that I hadn't seen him there of late because he hadn't been feeling well. When I asked him what was wrong, he told me the following story. He was on board an airplane in the Dallas/Fort Worth International Airport when he discovered that he had left his smartphone back in the American Airlines Admirals Club. The plane was still boarding, so he decided to get off the plane and run back to the club to fetch it. As anyone who has ever been in the Dallas/Fort Worth airport knows, it is enormous, and the terminals are interminable. My friend went running at full speed, found his phone on the table where he'd left it, and bolted back to the gate, where he found his plane departing. The door to the aircraft was now closed, so he was stuck in Dallas for another few hours. What was worse was that he had run through the airport—at least a mile, he was sure—on hard ground. He'd had a hip replacement and knew better than to run on any hard surface. As a result of his run, he'd put himself out of commission and had been unable to work out since returning. I told him how crazy the whole thing seemed and asked if he'd thought about just having the Admirals Club mail his phone back to him. And that was when he told me his version of crazy: he thought it was a no-brainer to run and get his phone, even with his hip and the missed flight. The idea that he should leave his phone behind with all its data seemed utterly insane to him. As he saw it, the consequences of his choice were well worth the outcome of reuniting with his phone.

I guess you could say, then, that these two friends are the mother and father of this detox program, inspiring me not only to foster awareness but also to chart a path from awareness to action!

Tech addiction is not just an idea, and it's no longer just for teenagers or porn aficionados. It's here, it's real, and it's taking over our lives. Like any addiction, there comes a point when we reach a level of disappointment, agitation, despair, or whatever negative emotion becomes intolerable and we know that we need to change. We finally get that if we want our lives to be different, we have to behave differently. As challenging and painful a place as this is to inhabit, it is also a place of great power and possibility.

Before you begin the 30-Day Tech Detox I've developed, I would like you to take the following preparatory steps.

STEP 1   Create a log.

Choose one workday or a full workweek, as well as one weekend, to track your use of all tech devices.

- Log the total amount of time you spend with them and the number of times you check them—even the briefest phone checks.

- Note the sorts of activities you engage with and whether they are work related or personal.

- Note whether or not your tech activity was necessary.

- Notice and record your mood and what the situation was when you got on. For example, were you bored? Were you agitated? Was there a lull in the day? Were you working?

- Note the way you felt when you got off. Did you feel tired, amped up, excited, overwhelmed?

If creating a log gets in the way of your initiating the detox or you're more than ready to get started and don't want to wait any longer, then skip the log and go straight to action. Whether or not you create the log, do determine the number one behavior you want to cut down on or eliminate, which may involve multiple devices.

STEP 2 Find a partner for your detox.

Commit to contacting each other every day during the thirty days to check in on your program and to be available to each other if your detox feels threatened. If partnering with someone isn't possible, then simply tell someone about your issue with technology and your plan to detox. Sharing this with another person will help make you accountable for your behavior and for sticking with the detox.

STEP 3 Contemplate.

Complete the following:

- Identify five negative consequences of your technology use.

- Identify five positive results that will come from cutting down or changing your technology use.

- How do you want to feel when your detox is complete?

- How do you want your life to be different at the end of these thirty days?

- What is your deepest aspiration in committing to this detox?

STEP 4   Support yourself.

Write the following statements down on index cards or sticky notes and post them around your computer, office, home, and car interior. I've grouped them into three categories, which move you from desire to intention to action.

1. I want to be in control of my choices around technology.
   I want my relationship with technology to change.
   I want my life to change.

Whenever you read these statements, spend some time with them; marinate in them, one at a time. Go to a deeper place than inside your head. Really feel in your heart the personal truth and meaning in these words.

2. If I want my relationship with technology to change, if I want to feel different in my life, then I need to change how I am behaving and what I am doing in my life.

Sit with this statement for a few minutes whenever you read it and contemplate its truth.

(**3**) I am now deciding and committing to behaving differently
so that I can feel different.

Sit quietly with this declaration. Let the power of this profound decision take up residence in your heart and mind. Invite yourself to fully experience and own the promise that you are making to yourself.

STEP 5 Move your computer to a less comfortable place in your home.

STEP 6 Buy a new journal for this detox.

At the end of each day throughout this 30-day detox, write down something (length is unimportant) about your experience with the process. You can write about anything you're experiencing: a new behavior introduced on a particular day, an insight the day revealed, a general account of a day in detox, or anything else about you and your efforts to get free from tech addiction.

⏻

Congratulations! You have taken the first steps on your road to freedom.

Two more things before you begin your detox. First, remind yourself that you are breaking an addiction or, at the least, a very strong habit. More than anything else, this requires the willingness to just say no—to stop what you are doing and the way you have been doing it. You can't break an addiction or a habit without being willing to make this choice and to take the action of stopping. Now is the time you have committed to detoxing, which means now is the time you have committed to stopping. Next, at the end of the daily detox instructions, you will find a section titled "Sense Pops." Review and use this section in tandem with the 30-day detox. It gives you useful tips for getting out of your head and reconnecting with your senses and the present moment.

The 30-Day Tech Detox is cumulative—with each new prescription, you will continue to practice the previously prescribed actions. So, for example, on day 5, you will be practicing five new behaviors, the behavior of day 5 and those from days 1, 2, 3, and 4. By day 30, you will be practicing thirty new behaviors. If a prescription doesn't apply to that particular day (for example, "Refrain from use during exercising"), switch it with a day when it does. Now, the important part: action!

30-Day Tech Detox

DAY 1   Pay attention to and internally note every time you feel the impulse or hear the thought to check one of your devices or computer. When you notice this, ask yourself, "Am I checking out of habit?" and "Is this checking necessary right now?" (For example, is it necessary for work?) If the answer is "Habit" or "Not Necessary," then repeat to yourself, "Stop" and do just that.
Simultaneously, designate three times in the day when you are allowed to check your device, whether necessary or not.

DAY 2   Refrain from any tech use when socializing or otherwise interacting with people (except at work, if needed). This includes everyone—shopkeepers, waiters, and service people, as well as your family and friends.

DAY 3   Refrain from holding your device in your hand or keeping it in your pocket when it's not in use. Store it out of sight elsewhere.

DAY 4   Refrain from using any of your devices during the first hour after you wake up in the morning.

If your smartphone is also your alarm clock, treat it as such. Turn it completely off as soon as it's sounded your morning wake-up.

DAY 5   Refrain from using tech devices during the last hour before you go to bed.

DAY 6   Turn off all alerts and notifications on your device. If your cell phone is your alarm clock, leave only the alarm notification intact.

DAY 7   Refrain from using your devices on public transportation or in taxis.

DAY 8   Write down four activities or experiences that nourish your spirit. Keep these simple and accessible—not the climbing-to-the-summit-of-Mount-Everest sort. Give yourself one of these experiences today, and get one on the calendar for each week to come. This practice should continue weekly after your detox as well.

DAY 9   Refrain from using your devices while waiting in line—any kind of line.

DAY 10   Refrain from using technology in the car, except when you need GPS assistance.

DAY 11   Refrain from using while waiting for something to begin, such as a movie, a play, a concert, or a social interaction.

DAY 12   Refrain from using during events—for example, at concerts, the theater, or children's recitals.

DAY 13   Make your bathroom a tech-free zone.

DAY 14   Refrain from using technology while walking on the street.

DAY 15   Make your bedroom (or bedroom area, if you live in a studio) a tech-free zone. Remove all devices and computers and refrain from using in the room or area where you sleep.

DAY 16   Set aside two continuous three-hour blocks of time in the day when you will be tech free. This can be scheduled on a weekend day if it is impossible during the workweek.

DAY 17   Refrain from using while exercising, unless you are providing yourself with music.

DAY 18   Refrain from immediately using the Internet to research non-work-related information that you have forgotten or want to know—for example, looking up the name of a television actor or the year a song was released. Wait at least twenty-four hours before going online to find out the answer, if the answer hasn't already occurred to you.

DAY 19   If there is a website that is particularly addictive for you, sign up for Net Nanny or another service that prevents you from accessing it.

DAY 20   Refrain from tech use while cooking and eating.

DAY 21   Refrain from using when walking or being in nature.

DAY 22   Commit to one tech-free day per month—the third Sunday of the month, for example. Now, enter these dates into your calendar for the rest of the year—and stick to them. Tell those close to you that you will not be available via your devices on that day of the month so that if they need to reach you about an urgent matter, they'll know why you're not electronically reachable. If necessary, provide children and others who may need to reach you with an emergency contact person on your "dry" days. Confirm with your backup person that they will be available.

DAY 23   Commit to going tech free on your next vacation, except when a specific matter, perhaps work related, absolutely requires tech access.

DAY 24   Refrain from using while interacting with your children. If you don't have children, refrain from use while with your pets (or plants).

DAY 25   Take a half-hour tech-free walk with no destination. Wander like a happy dog.

DAY 26   Spend ten minutes doing nothing—on purpose. Sit still, be quiet, listen to the sounds, feel your breath, experience the sensations in your body.

DAY 27   Send a handwritten letter, card, or note to someone you know. Express anything that feels important about your detox.

DAY 28   Do something in the "real" world that you would ordinarily do online—for example, call a friend instead of emailing them or go to the store to buy food or a magazine or a book.

DAY 29   Write down three things you are grateful for or happy about that are not tech based.

DAY 30   Make *this* moment matter, right now. Three times today, stop what you are doing and fully be where you are, sense your direct experience, allow things to be exactly as they are. Feel your own presence.

⏻

Notice how you feel at the end of this detox. Journal about your current experience. Consider these questions when you write:

- What feels different now?

- What's changed?

- How have you changed?

- What did you learn?

- What do you want to take forward?

- What is important about what you just did?

Congratulations! You did it. You completed the 30-Day Tech Detox. Spend a few minutes honoring the *you* who wants to live with awareness and wisdom rather than at the mercy of impulse or habit. You did something very difficult, not popular, and not commonplace in this era, all in the spirit of truly taking care of yourself. Acknowledge all the hard work you have done on this detox and how you have fulfilled this commitment to yourself, your life, and your freedom. Feel the strength that comes from deciding to show up for your own life!

⏻

Sense Pops

One of the real consequences of too much time with technology is that it disconnects us from our bodies and leaves us perpetually in our minds. Overfed with information and entertainment, we become disembodied heads, cut off from our senses and our physical reality, which then causes us to feel fragmented and uprooted. Our physical senses are what make us feel grounded and connected in the present moment. The senses are our portal into presence.

To counter this digital disembodiment, to feel your feet on the ground again and stay sane, try one or more of the following Sense Pops during each day of the detox program and thereafter. You'll find that paying attention to your senses in the simplest of ways can instantly land you back in your body and reestablish you where you are—in a grounded reality, out of the ether and in this here and now, where your body actually lives.

- Take three slow, deep breaths. Lengthen the inhalation and relax deeply with the exhalation. Feel the sensation of the breath from the inside out. Cultivate an intimacy with the sense of the breath. Feel the inhalation, the pause before the exhalation, the exhalation itself, and the pause before the next inhalation.

- Apply hand lotion and feel the sensations as you rub it into your hands. If the lotion is scented, inhale the fragrance and notice how that subtle scent affects your state of being.

- Apply a lip balm that feels good and maybe smells good, too. Feel the sensations on your lips. Enjoy the scent.

- Slowly roll your neck around in a circle in one direction and then back again in the other direction.

- Wiggle your toes, butterfly your knees, and rock your hips side to side. Feel the weight and presence of your lower body.

- Slowly roll each hand and each foot around in a circle and then back again in the opposite direction. Pay attention to the sensations.

- I call this one "Around the Body in Five Minutes." Do the full scan below to reconnect with yourself in the present moment.
  + Notice what you are hearing right now, with no judgment. Hear what you are hearing.
  + Notice what you are seeing right now, with no judgment. See what you are seeing.
  + Notice what you smell right now, with no judgment. Smell what you smell.
  + Notice what you taste right now, with no judgment. Taste what you taste.
  + Notice what your body is feeling, within and outside itself—the air, the clothing on your skin, whatever your body is touching, and the sensations inside your body. Notice without judgment. Experience what you are feeling.

- Make a cup of something hot and place your face over it. Feel the moisture and heat.

- Put your hands around a hot mug. For a minute, pay attention only to the sensation in your hands. Notice how the sensation changes throughout the minute.

- Rub a drop of peppermint or lavender oil on your pulse points and temples.

- Take a deep whiff of something with menthol or eucalyptus in it.

- Take a hot and damp hand towel and place it over your face. Do nothing but feel the sensations.

- Place both hands over your heart, one on top of the other. Feel the sensations that arise both in your hands and in your chest. Feel the breath moving in and out, the rising and falling of your chest, your heart beating, and the emotional sensations that arise.

- Take ten conscious, mindful steps. Pay close attention to the sensation in each foot as you place it on the ground, shift through from heel to toe, lift it off the ground, and place it down again.

- Place an ice cube at your third eye, the point just above and between your eyebrows. With your other hand, place a towel at your chin or nose. Feel the sensations of cold and wet as the ice melts down your face.

- Hug someone you love (or at least like). Hold the embrace a bit longer than you normally would. Feel the sensations that arise both inside and outside your body.

As you decrease your use of technology, it will be helpful and important to add activities to your day that involve the body. In addition to Sense Pops, begin or increase a physical exercise workout. Whether it's yoga, walking, dance, or another movement practice, physical exercise will assist your tech recovery process. Detoxing will free up a lot of energy that used to be directed toward your screens; this energy will need a place to land and be channeled. Moving your body is most useful for this purpose. It will help you anchor yourself in the physical and give your attention a new place to reside. In honor of your aspirations and actions, why not get up right now and give your recovery a shot of vitality? Move, dance, shake, rattle, roll, walk, stretch, swing, sway—do whatever your body longs to do. Feel and celebrate the freedom you are choosing to create!

notes

Introduction: Finding Ground in a Virtual World

1. "Stream of Consciousness: Shunryu Suzuki," GaiamLife.com, blog.gaiam.com/quotes/authors/shunryu-suzuki.

2. "Average Smartphone User Checks It Every Six Minutes—or 150 Times a DAY," *Daily Mail*, May 25, 2013, dailymail.co.uk/news/article-2330851/Your-smartphone-ruining-long-weekend-Average-user-checks-device-minutes--150-times-day.html.

3. Madlen Davies, "Average Person Now Spends More Time on Their Phone and Laptop Than SLEEPING, Study Claims," *Daily Mail*, March 11, 2015, dailymail.co.uk/health/article-2989952/How-technology-taking-lives-spend-time-phones-laptops-SLEEPING.html.

4. Chris Gayomali, "Jaw-Dropper: 18 to 24 Year Olds Average 110 Text Messages per Day," *TIME*, September 20, 2011, techland.time.com/2011/09/20/jaw-dropper-18-to-24-year-olds-average-110-text-messages-per-day/.

5. Andrew Soergel, "Could You Live without Your Smartphone?" *US News & World Report*, April 1, 2015, usnews.com/news/blogs/data-mine/2015/04/01/about-half-of-smartphone-owners-say-they-couldnt-live-without-it.

6. Henry Blodget, "90% of 18–29 Year Olds Sleep with Their Smartphones," *Business Insider*, November 21, 2012, businessinsider.com/90-of-18-29-year-olds-sleep-with-their-smartphones-2012-11.

Chapter 1: The Prison of Availability

1. Ian Sample, "Are Smartphones Making Our Working Lives More Stressful?" *Guardian US*, September 18, 2014, theguardian.com/technology/2014/sep/18/smartphones-making-working-lives-more-stressful.

2. David Volpi, "Heavy Technology Use Linked to Fatigue, Stress, and Depression in Young Adults," *Huffington Post*, August 2, 2012, huffingtonpost.com/david-volpi-md-pc-facs/technology-depression_b_1723625.html.

Chapter 4: Technoholics: A Generation of Addicts

1. Jennifer Van Grove, "Social Media Increases 'Cuddle' Chemical Production in the Brain," *Mashable*, June 25, 2010, mashable.com/2010/06/25/oxytocin-social-media/#wyYwaCVQcqqp.

2. Leslie Walker, "Self-Disclosure through Social Media Stimulates Brain Pleasure Centers," *About Tech*, personalweb.about.com/od/socialmediaaddiction/a/Self-Disclosure-Social-Media-Stimulate-Brains.htm.

3. "Tech Addiction Symptoms Rife among Students," *CBC News*, April 6, 2011, cbc.ca/news/technology/tech-addiction-symptoms-rife-among-students-1.994827.

4. Rachel Moss, "Social Media Addiction: Facebook and Twitter Beat Smoking as the Hardest Thing to Give Up," *Huffington Post UK*, August 20, 2014, huffingtonpost.co.uk/2014/08/20/social-media-addict-digital-detox_n_5693987.html.

5. Sahaj Kohli, "This Summer Camp Helps Adults Overcome Tech Addiction," *Huffington Post*, September 4, 2014, huffingtonpost.com/2014/09/04/this-summer-camp-helps-adults-get-over-their-tech-addiction_n_5762230.html.

6. Russ Warner, "Millennial Workers: Understand or Lose Them," *Huffington Post*, January 28, 2013, huffingtonpost.com/russ-warner/millennials-jobs_b_2566734.html.

7. Allison Stadd, "79% of People 18–44 Have Their Smartphones with Them 22 Hours a Day," *Adweek Blog Network's SocialTimes*, April 2013, adweek.com/socialtimes/smartphones/480485?red=at.

8. "Definition of Addiction," American Society of Addiction Medicine, April 19, 2011, asam.org/for-the-public/definition-of-addiction.

9. Delthia Ricks, "Study: Texting While Driving Now Leading Cause of Death for Teen Drivers," *Newsday*, May 8, 2013, newsday.com/news/nation/study-texting-while-driving-now-leading-cause-of-death-for-teen-drivers-1.5226036.

10. "Square-Eyed Britain: We Spend Average of 12 Hours a Day Staring at Screens," *Daily Mail*, May 27, 2011, dailymail.co.uk/news/article-1391417/Square-eyed-Britain-We-spend-average-12-hours-day-looking-screens.html.

11. Rachel Moss, "How Much Time Do We Spend on Our Devices? These Facts Show It's Time for a Digital Detox," *Huffington Post UK*, October 9, 2014, huffingtonpost.co.uk/2014/09/10/digital-detox-technology-addiction-facts_n_5795982.html.

Chapter 6: Information for Its Own Sake

1. "Wikipediholic," *Wikipedia*, January 14, 2016, en.wikipedia.org/wiki/
   Wikipedia:Wikipediholic.

2. Jean Piaget and Bärbel Inhelder, *The Psychology of the Child* (New York:
   Basic Books, 1969), 5-6.

Chapter 7: An Epidemic of Boredom

1. Jane McGonigal, "We Spend 3 Billion Hours a Week as a Planet Playing
   Video Games. Is It Worth It? How Could It Be MORE Worth It?" TED.
   com, "TED Conversations Archives," ted.com/conversations/44/we_
   spend_3_billion_hours_a_wee.html.

2. Valerie Strauss, "Beware the Quick Tech Fix When . . . ," *Washington
   Post*, September 13, 2012, washingtonpost.com/blogs/answer-sheet/post/
   is-technology-sapping-childrens-creativity/2012/09/12/10c63c7e-fced-
   11e1-a31e-804fccb658f9_blog.html.

3. Ibid.

4. Ibid.

Chapter 8: When Technology Bosses Us Around

1. Richard Whelan, ed. *Self Reliance: The Wisdom of Ralph Waldo Emerson as
   Inspiration for Daily Living* (New York: Three Rivers Press, 1991), 76.

Chapter 9: Our Phones Are Getting Smarter, but Are We?

1. "I Fear the Day That Technology Will Surpass Our Human Interaction,"
   QuoteInvestigator.com, quoteinvestigator.com/2013/03/19/tech-surpass/.

2. Nicholas Carr, *The Glass Cage* (New York: W. W. Norton, 2014), 57–58.

Chapter 10: Your Friend or Your Phone?

1. Helen Lee Lin, "How Your Cell Phone Hurts Your Relationships,"
   Scientific American, September 4, 2012, scientificamerican.com/article/
   how-your-cell-phone-hurts-your-relationships/.

Chapter 12: Last-Minute-itis

1. Kate Hakala, "There's a Modern Affliction Ruining Our Friendships—
   and We're All Guilty of It," *Connections.Mic,* March 18, 2015,
   mic.com/articles/113138/there-s-a-modern-problem-afflicting-our-
   friendships-and-it-s-time-to-talk-about-it#.MG9WAzKvs.

Chapter 14: A Remedy for Disconnection

1. "Attention Span Statistics," Statistic Brain Research Institute, April 2, 2015, statisticbrain.com/attention-span-statistics.

Chapter 16: Welcome to the Family, Smartphone

1. D. W. Winnicott, *Winnicott on the Child* (Cambridge, MA: Perseus Publishing, 2001), 38–40.

2. Rachel Moss, "Most Children Worry Their Parents Are Addicted to Their Phones and iPads, Survey Finds," *Huffington Post UK*, July 22, 2014, huffingtonpost.co.uk/2014/07/22/children-worried-parents-addicted-mobile-phones_n_5609510.html.

Chapter 19: The Umbilical Cord of Technology

1. Jason Gilbert, "WiFi, the Cloud Top Survey of Most Stress-Inducing Concepts in Digital: Virgin Digital," *Huffington Post*, July 24, 2012, huffingtonpost.com/2012/07/24/wi-fi-cloud-top-sress-in-tech-survey_n_1697987.html.

2. EC-Council, *Ethical Hacking and Countermeasures: Threats & Defense Mechanisms* (Clifton Park, NY: Cengage Learning, 2010), 2–3.

Chapter 21: Reawakening to the World We Share

1. Barry Tharaud, ed., *Emerson for the Twenty-First Century: Global Perspectives on an American Icon* (Newark: University of Delaware Press, 2010), 236.

Chapter 22: All Alone in Virtual Community

1. "Eric Whitacre's Virtual Choir—'Lux Aurumque,'" YouTube.com, youtube.com/watch?v=D7o7BrlbaDs.

2. Eric Whitacre, "A Choir as Big as the Internet," TED.com, March 2010, ted.com/talks/a_choir_as_big_as_the_internet.

3. Ibid.

4. Ibid.

5. Stephen Marche, "Is Facebook Making Us Lonely?" *The Atlantic*, May 2012, theatlantic.com/magazine/archive/2012/05/is-facebook-making-us-lonely/308930/.

6. Margie Warrell, "Text or Talk: Is Technology Making You Lonely?" *Forbes*, May 24, 2012, forbes.com/sites/womensmedia/2012/05/24/text-or-talk-is-technology-making-you-lonely/#421b8a7a436e.

7. "Connected and Disconnected: Technology, Empathy, and Loneliness," YouthVenture.org, February 24, 2014, youthventure.org/connected-and-disconnected-technology-empathy-and-loneliness.

8. Margie Warrell, "Text or Talk: Is Technology Making You Lonely?"

Chapter 25: Branding the Self

1. Catherine Pearson, "Social Media May Make Kids More Likely to Value Fame: Survey," *Huffington Post*, April 18, 2013, huffingtonpost.com/2013/04/18/social-media-kids_n_3111259.html.

Chapter 27: When Becoming Popular Is Our Purpose

1. LikesPlusMore.com, morefreefollowers.com/#sthash.gpncCQsZ.dpbs/.

2. Tweetangels.com.

Chapter 30: Finding Silence inside the Noise

1. Jacob Olesen, "Fear of Silence Phobia—Sedatephobia," Fearof.net, fearof.net/fear-of-silence-phobia-sedatephobia/.

2. Ibid.

Chapter 31: Making Time for Downtime

1. George Hofmann, "How Mindfulness Can Help Your Creativity," PsychCentral.com, October 5, 2013, psychcentral.com/blog/archives/2013/10/05/how-mindfulness-can-help-your-creativity/.

2. Les Fehmi and Jim Robbins, *The Open-Focus Brain* (Boston: Trumpeter, 2007), 51–54.

3. Ibid.

4. Travis Bradberry, "Multitasking Damages Your Brain and Career, New Study Suggests," *Forbes*, October 8, 2014, forbes.com/sites/travisbradberry/2014/10/08/multitasking-damages-your-brain-and-career-new-studies-suggest/#579c228d2c16.

5. Joel Stein, "Millennials: The Me Me Me Generation," *TIME*, May 20, 2013, time.com/247/millennials-the-me-me-me-generation/.

Epilogue: Freedom *In,* Not *From*

1. "Albert Einstein Quotes," BrainyQuote.com, brainyquote.com/quotes/quotes/a/alberteins390808.html.

about the author

Nancy Colier is a psychotherapist, interfaith minister, and spiritual counselor. She has a private practice in New York City and also leads groups and workshops on mindfulness in everyday life. Nancy guides her clients on the distanceless journey from the head to the heart, from the story of life to the direct experience of it. She is the author of *Getting Out of Your Own Way: Unlocking Your True Performance Potential* and *Inviting a Monkey to Tea: Befriending Your Mind and Discovering Lasting Contentment*, as well as a regular blogger for *Psychology Today* and the *Huffington Post*. Her work is based on nondual and Buddhist teachings, which she's been studying and practicing for more than two decades.

about sounds true

Sounds True is a multimedia publisher whose mission is to inspire and support personal transformation and spiritual awakening. Founded in 1985 and located in Boulder, Colorado, we work with many of the leading spiritual teachers, thinkers, healers, and visionary artists of our time. We strive with every title to preserve the essential "living wisdom" of the author or artist. It is our goal to create products that not only provide information to a reader or listener, but that also embody the quality of a wisdom transmission.

For those seeking genuine transformation, Sounds True is your trusted partner. At SoundsTrue.com you will find a wealth of free resources to support your journey, including exclusive weekly audio interviews, free downloads, interactive learning tools, and other special savings on all our titles.

To learn more, please visit SoundsTrue.com/freegifts or call us toll-free at 800.333.9185.

sounds true
many voices, one journey